HOUSE PLANTS
FOR FIVE
EXPOSURES

HOUSE PLANTS

FOR FIVE

EXPOSURES

George Taloumis

ABELARD-SCHUMAN
An Intext *Publisher*
NEW YORK   LONDON

NEW YORK	LONDON
Abelard-Schuman	Abelard-Schuman
Limited	Limited
257 Park Avenue So.	450 Edgeware Road W2 1EG
10010	and
	24 Market Square Aylesbury

Printed in the United States of America

CONTENTS

PART II
Ways and Means with Plants

INTRODUCTION

WHAT MAKES PLANTS GROW

Most people at one time or another try growing house plants. It is a prime source of pleasure for people who have no opportunity to garden outdoors; it also gives great enjoyment during the cold winter months to those who do have a garden. The sense of satisfaction and accomplishment is even greater if you nurse an African violet back to health, raise your own geraniums from cuttings, flower gloxinias and calla lilies from bulbs, and make root cuttings of coleus, patience plant, or Swedish ivy in water.

However, not everyone can raise house plants successfully. Why? The answer may rest in *exposure*.

In addition to soil, water, food, and humidity, plants need light—the right kind in the right amounts. Light is an element that has been widely explored by plant scientists in recent years, and we now know a great deal about it and the reaction of different kinds of plants to its degree of intensity.

Light for house plants comes through east, south, west, and north windows. A fifth exposure, which I have called *decorative*, involves, for the most part, subdued, reflected, or indirect light, with deficiencies made up by artificial illumination. Each of these five exposures—east, south, west, north, and decorative—differs in the amount and quality of light it receives, and each has the ability to support several kinds of house plants.

Until recently, most house plants were placed at or near windows, where they received maximum light for best growth. Today we place them anywhere we like, in any room of the house, at distances several feet from windows. No longer can you maintain that you cannot grow house plants because you live in a hot, dry, stuffy apartment. Even if your windows receive very little natural daylight, dracaenas, dumb canes, nephthytis, philodendrons, and pothos will survive for months on incredibly small amounts of light, natural or artificial, remaining ornamental even if they do not grow very much.

The first part of this book discusses the five exposures and plants that grow well in each. This does not imply, however, that these plants cannot be shifted to other exposures. Plants that do not require sunshine can easily be interchanged. You can do the same with those that need sun for best performance.

In the latter part you will find information about growing house plants, including soil mixtures, watering procedures, and methods of fertilizing, along with chapters on propagation, problems, and containers.

In this book we are primarily concerned with natural daylight plus that of incandescent lamp bulbs that are switched on at night for home use. The growing of plants entirely under artificial lighting is a whole new dimension, and is not covered in this book.

FOREWORD

Man feels the need for green growing things about him. The ancient Egyptians, Greeks, and Romans grew plants in containers outdoors, and often brought them indoors. The kinds of plants and the manner in which they were used differ from those of today. In the intervening centuries, the mode of living has changed, but the need for plants remains strong. Without them, the interiors of our homes would be less attractive.

The most artistic interiors, with costly, tasteful furnishings, somehow lack luster without the warmth of house plants. Just a few make the entire atmosphere of a home come to life. This is true, too, of unoccupied historic houses that are opened to the public as museums. There is no room in which house plants cannot be used to give a feeling of freshness and to dramatize bare spaces.

In today's homes, house plants are a part of the overall decor. Picture windows, stairways, vestibules, built-in planters, large expanses of wall—all these areas are planned specifically for house plants.

The most recent trend is to use plants in bathrooms. This started, perhaps, from the discovery that emaciated plants, brought there to benefit from the humidity created by showers and baths, revived astonishingly. Small bathrooms, as well as powder rooms, can be enlivened with a few healthy foliage plants. In spacious bathrooms, large foliage plants can be used to dramatize a corner or highlight a window. If the bathroom is poorly lighted, as many are in city apartments, plants with low light requirements can be chosen—plants such as dracaenas, ivies, nephthytis, philodendrons, pothos, and snake plants. Even without any natural daylight, they will stay fresh and green for several months, particularly if lights are kept on for some hours. Such plants—that is, plants used for decorative purposes—are expendable. They should be replaced when they are no longer attractive. Philodendrons on dim mantels or coffee tables cannot be expected to grow lushly. Dumb canes and ivies on sideboards will tolerate considerable abuse, but will not look hale and healthy indefinitely. Eventually it is time to make replacements.

Available today are plants to suit every need. Foliage plants from the jungles of Africa, Asia, and North and South America subsist on small amounts of light; cacti and succulents from desert areas can be grown in the dry atmospheres of overheated rooms, if given sun. Plant breeders and explorers are constantly introducing new variants and forms.

Small healthy plants can be used in place of cut flowers for a dinner party or other occasion. Flowering African violets arranged on a tray for the dining room table are lovely when illuminated by candle light. Blooming geraniums or orchids, pots of parsley, chives, or other herbs from sunny kitchen windows, bromeliads in all their variation of leaf form, spathiphyllums with pothos, flowering Christmas cactus with small-leaved English ivies, and other appealing combinations can be brought together from your house plant collection to be put on display for special occasions.

Although there are today excellent artificial flowers and potted plants—tulips so real they have to be touched, flowering African violets and geraniums, potted cut-leaved philodendrons with leaves that do not turn yellow—nothing can take the place of living house plants. They are very much with us, and they are definitely here to stay.

History of House Plants

Few of us know much about the history of house plants. As we grow older we recall the plants of our childhood, the kinds that mother and grandmother grew. We always had rubber plants that grew so big they touched the ceiling. When taken outdoors for the summer, the leaves that had developed indoors scorched in the sun. We grew Boston ferns that invariably had scale, which my mother was unable to control in spite of frequent soap-and-water shampoos. When plants languished, they were always replaced. I also recall that we had what was called a "Belgian tree." It was supposed to be rare and tricky, and after a while it died. When I grew older, I learned that it was a Norfolk-Island-pine.

Withing the last 20 years I have seen many newcomers, among them aluminum plant (*Pilea cadieri*), donkey-tail (*Sedum morganianum*), Swedish ivy (*Plectranthus*), purple-leaved setcreasea, and flowering inch-plant (*Tradescantia blossfeldiana*). Today you can walk into almost any supermarket and pick up plants of blue or white browallia, black-eyed Susan vine (*Thunbergia*), or sensitive plant (*Mimosa pudica*).

It is always intriguing to pore over old books on house plants. The style of writing in olden days was florid and the mood sentimental. Many quotations from poetry were interjected in the text, but, of course, people had more leisure for reading and living than we do today. I derived infinite pleasure from a tiny volume, translated from the French by Cornelia J. Randolph of Virginia (1861), entitled *The Parlor Gardener, a Treatise on the House Culture of Ornamentals*. One chapter discusses appropriate plants for "the apartment." For mantels, hyacinths forced in water, blue hepaticas, and sweet-smelling *Vanilla tussilago* were recommended. Other popular house plants in that era included brunfelsia, camellia, heath, ixora, kennedia, and sparmannia. Many of these we do not know and are no longer available. I was amused by the double climbing violet that could be trained on a trellis and was commonly grown in Belgium and the north of France. There was emphasis on succulent plants, including crassula, mesembryanthemum, opuntia, and stapelia. One section discussed gardening on balconies in summer. And according to that book, both warm and cold portable greenhouses were available.

Terrariums

Another old book, *Window And Parlor Gardening* by J. Jonsson-Rose (1895), treats of terrariums, describing plants to grow—filmy ferns, aroids, bertolonia, club-mosses, compact bromeliads, cypripedium orchis, fittonia, marantas, pellionia, and peperomias. It deals with the culture of such bulbs as eucharis, hymenocallis, crinum, zephyranthes, and *Imantophyllum miniatum*, known today by its new botanical name, *Clivia miniatum*. Listed as "popular florist flowers" are balsam, begonias, calceolaria, cineraria, Chinese primula, cyclamen, fuchsia, stock, wall flowers, geraniums, heliotrope, marguerite or Paris daisy, and petunia, including double, raised from cuttings.

Other house plants of the day were flamingo plant (*Anthurium*), alocasia, variegated pineapple, flowering maple, sweet alyssum, veronica, agathis (reclassified *Felicia*), *Phyllotaenium lindeni* (*Xanthosoma*), boronia, eucalyptus, cigar plant (*Cuphea*), ruellia, allamanda, lantana, aspidistra, streptosolen, *Vinca rosea*, and yellow flax (*Linum trigynum*).

Another book, *Household Horticulture, A Gossip About Flowers* by Tom and Jane Jerrold (1881), devotes an entire chapter to "The Rose As a Window Plant," a flowering favorite that is little grown today. The rubber plant (*Ficus elastica*) was "the prince of window plants," hardy ferns were considered excellent, and daffodils, hyacinths, tulips, crocus, ixias, dwarf iris, and other Dutch bulbs were grown indoors. No household apparently was without primroses (*Primula*), and forced lily-of-the-valley seemed to grace every window sill. Other kinds of bulbs grown were: Scarborough lily (*Vallota*), Guernsey lily (*Nerine*), blue lily of the Nile (*Agapanthus*), orange and lemon plants, pomegranate, oleander, myrtle, calla, triteleia from America, heliotrope, and *Lilium speciosum*, considered "easy." Pages are devoted to "azaleas and tender rhododendrons."

Domestic Floriculture by F. W. Burbidge (1874) devotes considerable space to the so-called glazed or Wardian cases. These were the oldest types of terrariums—glass containers with adjustable glass on top in which many kinds of humidity-loving plants were grown. Fernery, bottle garden, crystal garden, and glass garden were other names by which they were known.

I was particularly fascinated by Edwin A. Johnson's *Winter Greeneries At Home* (1878) because it lists the most common reasons for pot plant failures. Basically, the causes are the same today:

1 - Too much water
2 - Too little water
3 - Too much or not enough sunshine
4 - Too hot
5 - Too cool
6 - Lack of nutrients
7 - Pots too small
8 - Pots too large
9 - Sudden changes in temperature or drafts

One interesting deduction: Almost all of the unusual plants grown indoors in former years required cool growing conditions. Central heating was lacking, and houses in England and other western European countries were warmed by open fires. Hence it is not extraordinary that novelties such as heaths, hepaticas, lily-of-the-valley, violets, heliotrope, primroses, and hardy ferns were a part of every household.

PART I

The Five Exposures

(1)

East-Facing Windows

Windows that face the rising sun are ideal for house plants. Many consider it the perfect exposure, with enough sunshine for sun-loving plants if they are placed close to windows. Yet morning sun, less intense than noontime and afternoon sun, is even suited to some shade-tolerant foliage plants.

There is a quality of magic about the east, where the sun first appears over the horizon to start each new day. Little wonder that the sun, as a life-giving force, has been worshiped by diverse peoples the world over. In Stockholm, Sweden, where days are short in winter and long in summer, an impressive bronze figure of a man by the well-known sculptor, Carl Milles, greets the rising sun with outstretched arms as he overlooks the Grand Canal. Some kinds of trees even lean sharply toward the east, as if drawn by a magnet, among them the Australian pine (*Casuarina*) of southern gardens and the cottonwood of the north.

The impact of eastern exposure on house plants depends on the amount of direct sunshine it gives the plants. If there are adjacent buildings, the light is lessened, the amount depending on how close and how tall the buildings are and whether they shut out the sun in winter, yet allow it to enter in summer, when it is higher in the sky. These are factors that play determining roles.

Also to be considered is the presence of trees, their proximity and size, and whether they are evergreen or deciduous. Evergreen trees remain the same all year round, except that they grow a little each season, thus gradually casting larger areas of shade. Deciduous trees allow winter sunshine to enter windows through their naked branches, but in summer they cast heavy shade. Some, like the sugar maple, come into leaf early; others, like American ash and honey-

3

locust, leaf much later. Porches, balconies, and broad eaves, which are characteristic of many contemporary houses, influence house plant growth. Windows opening on to porches that face east usually receive full sunshine when the sun is rising, in both summer and winter.

Unobstructed East

If you have east windows that look out on the street or you live on an upper floor in a city apartment, your east windows probably receive full sun. If your windows face northeast, they belong to this category. True, they are subjected to much less sunshine, but in summer when the sun rises in the northeast, the difference is not great.

The rising sun bathes plants in its rays. As the sun moves slowly higher and southward, plants get less and less sun. First deprived are plants located several feet away from the windows, and last to benefit from the sun's rays are those on window sills. The time of year, of course, makes a difference. In summer the sun rises in the northeast and moves up quickly into the sky; in winter it rises in the southeast and retains its low position, so that its rays reach farther into rooms. Winter sun from the east is mild and gentle, a wonderful life-giving force for practically all kinds of house plants.

Day Length Varies

Latitude plays a significant role. The farther north you go, the shorter the days become in winter and the longer they are in summer. This, of course, influences plant growth and behavior. Also the farther north you live, the lower the position of the sun in the sky, in both summer and winter, as compared with the warm areas of the globe.

The morning sun becomes hotter as it moves up in the sky. It starts out "cool," and even in the heat of summer it is not as hot as midday or afternoon sunshine. It is beneficial for plants to be greeted with a gentle warmth, but when the sun becomes too hot (mostly in summer), it will scorch the leaves.

A great variety of plants can be grown in east windows, both flowering and foliage. Occasionally, adjustments must be made to protect some plants from too much sun or to give others a little more sun, but in general these are plants that will enjoy good health in an eastern exposure.

4

Achimenes

(Achimenes)

This tuberous plant, related to the African violet, is a dainty trailer, often grown in hanging baskets and window boxes outdoors in the South. Heat-loving (its Greek name means "suffers from cold"), it has simple, oval leaves and striking tubular flowers in blue, scarlet, pink, and white. Well-known varieties are Purple King, Pink Beauty, Violetta, Margaret, Celestial, Mauve Queen, and Pure White.

Start the tiny tubers in trays in early spring, at 70° to 80° F., in a mixture of moist peatmoss and sand, shifting young plants, to permanent containers when a few inches high. Tubers can also be planted directly in pots. Space three to five tubers in a four-inch, five to seven in a six-inch, and 10 to 12 in a twelve-inch pot. Use soil recommended for African violets.

Achimenes are excellent flowering plants for shade. Place outdoors when danger of frost is over. Start to feed with liquid fertilizer when six inches high, continuing every two or three weeks while plants are in flower. Withhold water gradually when leaves show signs of withering in fall, and cut stems to base when tops have dried. Tubers can be lifted and stored in peatmoss at 60° F., never lower than 50° F., or they can be left in their pots. Sprinkle occasionally to prevent shriveling, and start into growth again in early spring.

Small bulbs that develop at axils of leaves in early fall may be gathered, stored, and planted in moist sphagnum moss in spring for new plants. Since achimenes dislike cold, they should be protected from strong winds in summer. They combine attractively with fuchsias, wax begonias, coleus, patience plants, and thunbergias (black-eyed-Susan-vine) in window boxes in shade.

African Violet

(Saintpaulia)

Next to philodendron, African violet is the most widely grown of all house plants. Certainly, it is the most common of flowering pot plants, even more popular than geranium.

Compact in form, requiring little space, African violets (not true violets, but members of the genus *Saintpaulia*) are easily accommodated on narrow window sills and glass plant shelves, flowering in small amounts of light.

African violets are warmth-loving plants, suited to wintertime indoor temperatures that are 70° F. and above. Though native to humid tropical jungles, they are tolerant of dry air. African violets grow quickly, even from leaf cuttings, reaching flowering size in a short time, and are available in a surprising variety of forms, single and double, in colors including purple, violet mauve, rose pink, red, and white.

African Violet Society

There are thousands upon thousands of admirers of the African violet throughout the country. The national African Violet Society, to which many of these enthusiasts belong, publishes a handsome magazine and has numerous regional clubs that stage shows several times a year. Enthusiastic devotees collect and grow hundreds of plants in their homes, often in small city apartments. Deeply imbedded in the American way of life, the African violet is here to stay, and an equally good substitute would be hard to come by.

Yet, African violets have their troubles. Too much watering results in rotting; insufficient watering causes plants to wilt and grow poorly. Cold water produces spots on the leaves, and a high-nitrogen fertilizer promotes lush foliage with few flowers. Aphids, mealy bugs, cyclamen mites, and other pests and diseases take a toll, while the slightest presence of artificial cooking gas makes blossoms drop.

Success with African violets depends largely on the right kind of soil. This is easily obtained commercially in the form of a mixture that is suited to other plants with fine, fibrous root systems, including all kinds of begonias and African violet relatives known as gesneriads.

You can make your own mixture with equal amounts of garden loam, leafmold or peatmoss, and sand. Add to this bonemeal or superphosphate, one teaspoon to each quart of mixture. Another combination consists of one part good loam, one part sand, two parts leafmold or peatmoss, and one-half part dried manure. Yet another comprises four parts loam, four parts leafmold or peatmoss, two parts sand or perlite, one part dried manure, plus the bonemeal or superphosphate.

6

First sterilize the loam by baking in the oven or by pouring boiling water over it before adding the other ingredients.

Some enthusiasts have their own formula. A couple I once interviewed uses soil from a compost pile, which they sterilize in the oven in a covered roasting pan for an hour at 250° F. After spreading the soil on a plastic sheet in the basement for a week to aerate, one part each of Canadian sphagnum peat, vermiculite, and perlite are added. Into 15 gallons of the mixture goes one pint of dried manure, one gallon of charcoal, and two ounces each of bonemeal, superphosphate, and a 5–10–10 fertilizer (5 parts nitrogen, 10 parts phosphorous, 10 parts potash), plus two tablespoons each of chlordane and captan. The formula is used for all gesneriads.

African violets can be fed with an ordinary balanced fertilizer, like 5–10–5 or 4–12–4, which should be applied as a liquid to moist soil; otherwise leaves will turn yellow. Also available are special-formula foods. The appearance of small blooms indicates that plants are going into their resting period.

Much controversy exists as to whether plants should be watered from above or below. Some swear by one method, some prefer the other; both produce successful results. In either case, use room temperature or lukewarm faucet water; cold water chills plants and causes markings on the leaves. If watering from top, keep water away from crowns, as this may induce rotting, particularly during long periods of cloudy or rainy weather.

The sunshine of early morning or late afternoon is generally best. In winter, south exposure is not too strong, but move plants when sun becomes hotter or temper the sun's rays with fine curtains or other screening, such as Venetian blinds. African violets also grow magnificently all year round in north windows. In dull winter weather, plants will perk up and flower better if placed near or under 100-watt incandescent lamps for several hours each day. Turn pots at least once a week to keep rosettes well rounded, and remove dust with a soft camel's hair brush. Too much dust cuts down on amounts of light, and results in fewer blossoms. Sprinkling foliage periodically or giving plants a warm shower will also remove dust and satisfy the need for humidity. Allow plants to dry in shade; if placed in sun, leaves will spot.

To propagate, select the middle leaves, since the outer are hard and tend to rot. With a sharp knife, cut the stem close to the crown, without leaving a stub. Make a new cut, at an angle, so the stem is about an inch and a half long, and set aside for an hour to seal. To root in water, spread a piece of aluminum foil over a small glass filled with water. Make a hole in the center of the foil, and insert the stem. If a portion of the leaf touches water, it will rot. Leaf cuttings can also be

7

rooted in damp vermiculite or perlite, but usually take longer. When roots develop (from 14–21 days), plant in two-and-one-quarter-inch pots, shifting to the three-inch size after the first flowering. Single crowns are the ideal; divide and repot plants with more than one. Give your African violets a summer vacation, when all danger of frost is over, preferably on porches, under laths, or in secluded terrace corners, sheltered from strong sun and wind and driving rains. Pots can be plunged in the open ground under large shrubs; water and feed as you do your other house plants.

Aerosol bombs, especially prepared for African violets, will control aphids, mealy bugs, red spider and cyclamen mites. Keep the container 12 to 18 inches away to prevent "burning," using quick one-second bursts and a rotary motion.

A difficulty known as stem or petiole rot will sometimes show up. Not a disease, it occurs when stems of outer leaves touch the rims of pots—particularly clay pots. You can prevent this by covering rims of pots with aluminum foil or cellophane tape. Stem rot can also be avoided by a cardboard collar, dipped in paraffin, placed around each crown.

For displaying, start to disbud at least five to six months in advance, removing all suckers—that is, new shoots that develop around the base of plants. Double blossoms last longer than singles and do not shed petals. They are generally preferred. Blue Boy, Blue Girl, and Orchid Beauty are blue-lavender. Pinks include the double Strawberry Shortcake, Pink Arabian, Pride of Rochester, and the unusual variegated Lilian Jarret. Other worthwhile varieties are the red-violet Redhead, the pink-and-green Dawn, the deep rose and white Wintry Rose, the white and lavender Doll Dance, and the blue Charm Song. Good whites are White Lady, Wedgewood, and Winter Magic.

Azalea

(Rhododendron)

A popular gift plant from Christmas to Mother's Day, azalea is a shrub that makes a permanent house plant. Colorful when in full bloom, new florist plants usually have several buds that will open if kept in a cool, sunny window. Azaleas require water constantly; otherwise leaves will turn yellow and drop. In clay pots, they may need watering twice

Azalea and paper white narcissus

Gloxinia

9

a day. Mist spray the foliage, or give your plant a shower with tepid water in the sink or bathtub.

Usually, new azaleas do not need repotting for two or three years. Transfer when potbound after flowering, using a soil of four parts loam, three parts sand, one part leafmold or peatmoss, and one-half part dry manure. Prepared azalea soil may also be purchased. When the plant is making new growth, feed it with acid fertilizer, which is also recommended for camellias and gardenias. Yellowish foliage, often due to lack of iron, is easily corrected with micronized iron.

Place azaleas outdoors in spring in light shade, plunging pots in open ground if possible. Water and feed regularly, and cut back long shoots to keep plants shapely. However, avoid severe pruning. If red spider mites turn leaves yellow-gray, spray with kelthane. In fall bring indoors to a cool spot, perhaps a bedroom where a window is opened at night, but move to the living-room when flowering starts.

Azaleas used as house plants include Pink Pearl, Lavender Queen, Snow, and Salmon Beauty. These varieties are not hardy outdoors in the North.

Begonias

(Begonia)

As a group, begonias have long been favorites, and comprise hundreds of species and varieties, all members of the genus *Begonia*. The American Begonia Society, one of the largest specialized plant groups, has members in all parts of the country.

Begonias like humidity, yet tolerate dry air. However, they insist on rich, humusy, well-drained soil: equal parts loam, sand or vermiculite, and peatmoss or leafmold, plus a sprinkling of mixed fertilizer and superphosphate.

I find that most begonias grow best in the weak sun of the early or late part of the day; hot noonday sunshine makes leaves reddish and coarse in texture. Give plants warmth, 70° F or higher, and keep soil moist to prevent the fine roots from drying out. Pinch and prune as needed, turning pots around occasionally for symmetrical growth. In winter, avoid placing on cold, drafty window sills. Cuttings root easily in a mixture of sand and peatmoss.

Most widely grown is the wax or semperflorens begonia. Since it is constantly in bloom, it is also called Busy Lizzie. Among other kinds

Rex begonia

are the beafsteak begonia (*B. feasti*), with rounded, shiny, bright green leaves, reddish beneath. Angel Wing has large, irregularly shaped leaves and clusters of rose flowers. The recently introduced *B. richmondensis*, already common in hanging baskets outdoors, has showy pink blossoms and leaves edged with red.

Rex begonias are admired for the metallic markings on their leaves. They include such well-known varieties as Louise Closson, purple bronze on dark green; Jule Chretien, rose-pink sprinklings on green; and Glory of St. Albans, rose highlighted with silver sheen.

One of the most temperamental of all is the calla begonia, so called because the new white leaves resemble miniature calla lilies. for years it has been grown successfully in farmhouses in northern New England, where atmosphere is cool and dry. Avoid overwatering and too much sunshine; summer heat and high humidity are its enemies.

Bird-of-Paradise

(Strelitzia reginae)

This bold-leaved South African plant, with odd, multihued blossoms, is ideal for a large room in a contemporary house, with windows that reach from ceiling to floor. A member of the banana family, it has long-lasting, orange-yellow flowers, each accented by a blue "tongue," like a bird-of-paradise alighting to rest. Before Americans traveled as much as they do now, bird-of-paradise was a curiosity plant at flower shows.

Strelitzia is commanding even when not in bloom. Its leathery, strongly veined, dark green leaves, one and a half feet long and one-half foot wide, appear on strong, three-foot-high stems. Flowers develop when plants have ten leaves or more. Started from seed, they require at least three years to reach this stage.

Bird-of-paradise needs a large pot and eventually a wooden tub. Give it a regular potting mixture, and let it rest from October through January, keeping soil on the dry side, at 55° to 65° F. As days lengthen in February, bring it into a warmer atmosphere, start to water more liberally, and feed with liquid fertilizer.

Transfer small plants to larger containers as needed, preferably in spring, but repot large plants after blossoms fade. Divisions taken from mother plants after flowering will produce new plants. Several large specimens in redwood tubs present a dramatic sight on the terrace in summer.

Episcia

(Episcia)

If you are an African violet addict, chances are you grow episcia, a relative that requires similar care. A tropical trailing plant, with heavily marked leaves and small, showy flowers, it makes a superb hanging basket plant.

The simple leaves, shaped like those of African violets, vary from four to six inches in length, and may be green and silver, creamy-white

Episcia

and brown, or green and brown. Foliage remains attractive at all times, and flowers appear mostly during the spring and summer months. Plants like humidity and warmth, 70° to 75° F., and become chilled at below 55° F. Grow in a light, humusy soil or an African violet mixture.

For startling effects, combine in one pot two or three kinds for variety of foliage and flowers—scarlet, orange, rose, pink, or white. Plants stay compact if kept pruned constantly. Keep soil moist, but not wet, as this rots the fine roots. When plants are growing actively feed them with weak liquid fertilizer every two or three weeks. Root cuttings in water to replace old plants.

Growers offer well over fifty varieties, for the collector Commonly grown are *Episcia fulgida*, known as the "red flame violet," and the orange *E. cupreata*, both ideal for hanging baskets. *E. splendens*, a strong grower with emerald-green and silver leaves, has red flowers. Other worthwhile varieties are Silver Sheen, silver and green; Mrs. Fanny

Haage, green and bronze, and Chocolate Soldier, green, silver, and brown. The unusual *E. dianthiflora* has small, dark green, velvety leaves on trailing stems. Its white fringed flowers, as its botanical name suggests, resemble the garden pink (*Dianthus*).

False Aralia

(*Dizygotheca elegantissima*)

Also called finger aralia, this graceful, airy foliage plant contrasts dramatically when placed near bold-leaved kinds. Sometimes listed as *Aralia elegantissima*, it is a member of the aralia family, native to the New Hebrides islands in the Pacific. False aralia has an upright habit and spreading leaves made up of seven to 11 thin, wavy, ribbon-like leaflets, like the outstretched fingers of a hand. They are dark reddish-copper in color, with petioles blotched white.

When plants grow old, they lose their lower leaves and become leggy, resembling small palms. Tip cuttings can be rooted in peatmoss and sand. They are effective when several are grown in a single pot. Insufficient light, dry air, and over- or underwatering cause leaves to drop. Otherwise, plants respond to average care. Give sun and 60° to 70° F. temperatures.

The less known *D. veitchi* from New Caledonia has narrower, toothed leaflets, one-fourth of an inch wide, green above and reddish beneath. More slender are the leaflets of *D. v. gracillima*, accented with white midribs.

Polyscias balfouriana, another member of the aralia family, also makes a good house plant. Often listed as *Aralia balfouriana*, it grows several feet high in its native New Caledonia, but remains smaller as a pot plant. Light green leaves, like those of geranium, are coarsely toothed and blotched with white along the margins. Give a humusy soil, a moist atmosphere, and keep well watered when growing actively. It remains compact, with leaves close to the base. In warm areas, as in Florida, *Polyscias balfouriana* is a common hedge plant.

Gloxinia

(Sinningia)

Few flowering pot plants are more striking than gloxinia. A popular summer florist plant, many indoor gardeners prefer to raise their own, aiming either at summer or winter bloom.

Gloxinia is a warmth-loving bulbous plant, with large, velvety leaves and tubular flowers, frequently bicolored, varying from deep purple and maroon to purest white, and including rose and pink, lavender, blue, and bright red. Like African violet, it is a member of the gesneriad family, which includes columneas, streptocarpus, achimenes, episcias, kohlerias, isolomas, smithianthas, and chiritas. All require the same soil mixture.

A gloxinia that comes from a florist shoud be placed in a bright window, where it will bloom for several weeks. Keep the soil moist, and give the plant fresh air in summer. Cut off old blossoms and yellow leaves. After flowering, these plants go into a normal rest period, indicated by yellowing, withering leaves. Cut down on watering gradually, and store the bulbs, leaving them in their pots, in the basement or other storage place at 50° to 55° F. Temperatures below 45° F. are harmful. Water the bulbs occasionally to prevent shriveling.

The same tubers, or new ones, can be started in February or March for summer flowering. Several bulbs may be started in trays in an equal mixture of peatmoss and sand to be transferred to individual pots after sprouts appear. Or tubers can be started directly in pots. Use a five-inch pot for an average-sized bulb and the eight-inch size for an extra-large tuber. Place tubers with concave sides up, and barely cover with the medium. Keep moist, but avoid a soggy condition. Bulbs need little water until the tops make vigorous growth, but allowing soil to dry is damaging to the fine, fibrous root systems.

Keep at 60° to 65° F. at the start, giving 70 to 75° F. later. Young plants require strong light and some sun to prevent lanky growth. Feed them with liquid fertilizer when buds show color. If the plants are placed outdoors in summer, protect them from strong rains, hot sun, and wind, which tears the large, fleshy leaves.

For winter bloom, pot new bulbs in September or October instead of in the early spring. The same bulbs will not flower in summer and winter, as they need a rest. For new plants, root leaves taken from flowering plants in water or peatmoss and sand. Seed can be sown in a sandy, peaty mixture.

Golden Archangel

(Lamium galeobdolon variegatum)

I first saw this uncommon trailing plant in window boxes at a friend's house. Cuttings I was given rooted quickly in water, and made an excellent house plant in a sunny window all winter.

If you are familiar with the hardy ground cover called dead nettle (*Lamium maculatum*), which has blotched leaves, you will recognize this lamium; it is similar, with oval leaves heavily marked with silver. It resembles Swedish ivy (*Plectranthus*) in appearance, except that its leaves are smaller and hairy. Both are members of the mint family and have square stems.

A native of Europe and western Asia, golden archangel, named for its clusters of small yellow flowers, is hardy outdoors in New England. Yet it makes an undemanding house plant, growing well at average

Golden archangel

room temperatures. Give it an ordinary soil mixture, and keep it moist constantly, since it resents drying out. It requires sunshine; without sufficient amounts its growth is stringy and the leaves pale. Prune regularly to encourage branching.

In time, golden archangel will probably become as popular as Swedish ivy for hanging basket plants, indoors or out. It will also replace variegated vinca in window boxes, particularly if a dainty, less vigorous trailer is needed.

Japanese Euonymus

(Euonymus japonicus)

If you grow this shrubby evergreen, or one of its forms, chances are you acquired it from a florist's dish garden, with jade plant, peperomia, snake plant, and philodendron. The species, hardy in southern gardens, is little grown as a house plant, but its many colorful variations are.

One of the most appealing is the tiny-leaved Boxleaf euonymus (*E. j. microphyllus*), which has white along the leaf edges. It is compact and bushy, like the miniature-leaved *E. j. m. variegatus*. Other kinds to try are Gilt Edge (*E. j. aureo-marginatus*); and Yellow Eye (*E. j. mediopictus*). All are variations in green, yellow, and white. There are also the white variegated Silver Queen and the yellow variegated Golden Queen.

These euonymus make excellent house plants. They thrive best in a cool atmosphere under 60° F., but are still easy at higher temperatures if they are given sun and kept moist. All are upright, with rounded, glossy leaves. Use an average soil mixture, and keep moist, allowing the soil to dry a little between soakings. Feed plants when they are making new growth in spring, and prune and clip them to keep small and shapely. If scale appears, spray with malathion. Cuttings root easily in moist sand and peatmoss.

I have friends who grow several yellow variegated eunoymus in redwood tubs, which are kept in a cool, bright room in winter. In spring they are moved to the terrace and to bare spots in borders, where the tubs are set on bricks. They offer a pleasing change from geraniums, petunias, and other flowering plants that are grown in pots and other containers.

Orchid Cactus

(Epiphyllum)

With their long, arching, dark green stems (they are not leaves), orchid cacti are not particularly beautiful plants. But when their huge, satin-petaled blossoms with their showy yellow stamens unfold, they become as resplendent as the rose, peony, lily, or hibiscus. Some blooms may be as much as ten inches across.

In summer, orchid cacti are often seen in large tubs on porches or lawns of country houses. They are old-time plants, able to withstand much neglect, resting in winter, when they require very little water. Like orchids and Christmas cactus, they are epiphytes—that is, they grow in organic matter in the crotches of trees. They flower in the rainy season, and go dormant in the dry period. Pot plants usually bloom in summer.

Give orchid cactus the same soil as Christmas cactus. Keep as cool as possible in winter in a bright window, watering little and increasing the amounts as spring approaches. Feed these plants as new growth develops. Place them outdoors in partial shade in summer, and bring indoors early, as they are tender. Older plants spread several feet and take up a great deal of space, but they can be left in the same containers

Orchid cactus

for several years. Feeding with superphosphate aids blooming. Smaller plants are often grown in hanging baskets.

New plants can be rotted from cuttings six to ten inches long. Allow the cuttings to dry for a week to ten days to form calluses, as rooting will be better. Always keep them right side up, and insert the bottom end of each cutting in the rooting medium of peatmoss and sand. Stems of orchid cacti may be flat or three-angled.

Like Christmas cactus, plants are long lived. Large specimens a half century old, may sport over 200 blooms in a single season. Varieties are available in red, scarlet, pink, yellow, white, with lavender predominating. Unbelievably handsome are Sun Goddess, golden-orange with a ruby throat; Argus, apricot-pink; Madonna, ruffled white; Poinsettia, red; Pride of Bell, rose-orchid; and Ballerina, salmon-pink.

Closely related and similar in appearance is night-blooming cereus (*Hylocereus undatus*), with foot-wide white blossoms that open only at night. When large specimens come into full flower, friends and neighbors gather to enjoy the memorable event. The effect of a well-grown plant is like that of a display of fireworks.

Patience Plant

(*Impatiens sultani*)

In most books this plant is listed as patience plant, patience, or impatiens. Patient Lucy is yet another name for this free-flowering annual that makes a superb house plant in winter. The name impatiens means "impatient" and refers to the seed pods, which burst or explode if

Night-blooming cereus

touched when they are ripe. Since "impatient" and "patient" have opposite meanings, the latter is said to be an accidental variation.

For a section of the garden that is in partial or complete shade, patience plant is without peer, the conterpart of petunias or marigolds in full sun. A shrubby annual, with fleshy, light green stems and small, heart-shaped leaves, it has single, inch-wide, waxy blossoms in scarlet and crimson, lavender and purple, apricot, and pure white. The many hybrids are derivatives of *I. sultani* and *I. holsti,* and include tall, medium, and dwarf kinds. Recent introductions include the orange Park's Tangerine and A Go-Go, scarlet-red and white.

Patience plant succeeds in any kind of soil. Take cuttings from garden plants in late summer or pot up small specimens to grow indoors in winter. To flower, these plants need sun for part of the day. Keep them moist, feed moderately, and grow cool, if possible. Cuttings root quickly in water or peatmoss and sand. They may, in fact, be kept in water in jars all winter to plant outdoors in spring. Since patience plant is reputedly susceptible to lice, it is sometimes called Lousy Lucy.

Pilea

(Pilea)

My favorite pilea is aluminum plant (*Pilea cadieri*), a newcomer from the jungles of Vietnam. I remember that my first aluminum plant wilted badly when left on my desk at the Massachusetts Horticultural Society for the week-end. This happens to other pileas as well. They are low-growing foliage plants with small, insignificant flowers. They like warmth and humidity, and are good subjects for terrariums. Yet they make useful, slow-growing house plants, easily propagated by cuttings rooted in water.

Aluminum plant, also called watermelon pilea, has shiny, oval, dark green leaves, highlighted with silvery-gray on raised surfaces. It grows rather quickly and needs frequent pruning. Like all pileas, it likes a loose, humusy soil with good drainage, and a temperature of 65° to 75° F. with weak-sun in winter, shade in summer. A miniature form, *P. c. minimum,* has leaves blotched with silver.

The most common pilea before the advent of aluminum plant was the Mexican artillery plant (*P. microphylla*), a shrubby, fleshy-stemmed plant about a foot tall, with tiny, oval, light green leaves. It is often used outdoors to edge flower beds because it grows easily, and its fine, fern-like foliage contrasts with the larger leaves of other plants. It is called artillery plant because its ripe pollen discharges into smoky drifts when touched, reminiscent of the ripe seed pods of patience plant.

South American friendship plant (*P. involucrata*), which comes from Peru, has become a symbol to help promote friendship among the countries of North and South America. Also called panimiga, it is only six inches high, ideal for terrariums. Rough, oval leaves are dark green, marked with brown. Small pink flowers appear on top of the leaves. This pilea grows easily in a rich soil if kept moist, and can be increased by rooting tips in peatmoss and sand.

Rosary Vine

(*Ceropegia woodi*)

Heart-vine, hearts-entagled, and string-of-hearts are other provocative names for this interesting trailing plant that is prized for its religious symbolism. Small tubers, like rosary beads, appear in pairs at the axils of the small, heart-shaped leaves, along thin, stringy, pendulous stems that hang several feet on large specimens.

This member of the milkweed family, which makes an ideal hanging basket plant, is a never-failing curiosity when seen for the first time. Its fleshy, inch-long leaves are dark green, splashed with creamy-white or light green, marble-like in effect. Pinkish underneath, they become coppery in full sun. Small pinkish or purplish flowers, usually in pairs, appear along the wiry stems, which hang limply due to the weight of the succulent leaves.

Though indigenous to Natal in Africa, rosary vine is an adaptable house plant. Give it a light, well-drained soil, as recommended for cacti and succulents. Keep moist during the growing period, but allow it to dry out between waterings. If watering is decreased gradually, the plants will go dormant. Plant the tiny tubers to make new plants. Less known is the trailing or climbing *C. sandersoni*, which requires a trellis or other support on which to twine. Oval, grayish-green leaves, one-and-three-fourths inches long, are paired on thick, fleshy stems. Also native to Natal, its green and creamy-white flowers resemble parachutes in form. Culture is the same.

Star of Bethlehem

(Campanula isophylla)

Few house plants are more frustrating than this delicate beauty. Called also Italian bellflower, this native of Italy grows luxuriantly as a hanging basket plant in California, along with fuchsias and tuberous begonias. As a house plant, it is temperamental, but some indoor gardeners try it again and again.

To succeed indoors in winter, star of Bethlehem requires temperatures in the fifties. A true Canterbury bell, first cousin of the biennial and perennial kinds of northern gardens, it has small, oval, or heart-shaped leaves, gray-blue in the blue-flowering kind and light green in the white form. In a hanging basket, it cascades to about a foot, and

Star of Bethlehem

it flowers from August to November. Greenhouse techniques, which control light and temperature, bring it into flower at any time of year.

If you give Italian bellflower a cool, sunny window in an unheated room or hallway, it is an easy house plant. Keep plants moist when they are in full bloom. In early spring, when flowering is past, cut back the stems and repot, using a mixture of two parts soil, one part sand, one part leafmold or peatmoss, and one-half part dry manure. Throw in a handful of crushed limestone to each six-inch pot of soil. Make certain the drainage is good.

Water freely after repotting, and pinch new shoots to stimulate branching. Start to feed the plant in May, and continue to pinch until the middle of June. Plants may be taken outdoors in mid-June and should be placed in partial shade. When buds form in midsummer, feed the plants again with liquid fertilizer, preferably high in nitrogen. Bolster them with weak liquid fertilizer when they are in full bloom in fall or winter. Though star of Bethlehem withstands considerable cold in its native surroundings—even freezing—bring it indoors early so it can adjust to its new environment.

(2)

Sunny South Windows

A southern exposure receives sunshine "all day long," for a duration of six hours or more. Like an eastern exposure, it imparts an element of magic, and is warm, bright, cozy, shielded in winter from cold north winds. Warmth- and sun-loving plants are recommended for this exposure. As with all exposures, nearby buildings and trees influence the amount of light. The time of year and the position of the sun also affect the light of a southern exposure. In summer, south windows receive very little direct sunshine; in winter it streams in abundantly. It saturates furniture and furnishings. Walls reflect its shimmering rays. All is bright and cheery, suffused in pure golden-yellow light.

Winter sun is not hot. For weeks around December 21, the shortest day of the year, African violets, ferns, philodendrons, and other shade-tolerant foliage plants can be placed at south windows. When the sun becomes hotter, in late February and March, leaves of shade-loving plants may burn. Some turn reddish or yellowish, as does African violet, philodendron, and Swedish ivy. On the other hand, plants with colored leaves, such as coleus, bloodleaf, zebrina, and velvet plant, take on their most intense colorings if given full sun in spring.

South exposure is fascinating. It has several variations, from full sunshine in winter to virtual shade in summer, with heat in spring and fall because the sun in winter is low in the sky; in summer, high. It is the ideal exposure for indoor living; in winter you get abundant sunshine, when you want and need it, but in summer, when it is unwanted, it almost vanishes. The following plants grow well in a southern exposure.

25

Blood-leaf

(Iresini herbsti)

For a sunny window, nothing is more heart lifting than this cheerful plant. At midday, when strong sun strikes its translucent leaves, it glows radiantly, and is more colorful than geraniums, coleus, or bougainvilleas. Sunshine, however, is needed to bring out the full color intensity of the foliage.

A member of the amaranth family, blood-leaf, also called beefsteak plant, is native to South America. Its name is actually misleading, since the leaf coloring is not blood-red, but rather purple-red. This bushy plant, which trails as it grows larger, has leaves that may be four or five inches long when grown outdoors. Indoors, of course, they are smaller. Notched at the tips, the leaves have veins that are prominent and greenish-yellow in color. Stems, like the leaves, are red. Variety *I. h. aureo-reticulata* has green leaves, highlighted with yellow veins. The two kinds offer contrast when grown side by side.

I. lindeni has pointed leaves, more red than magenta, and a more pyramidal growth habit. Both, commonly used for bedding in parks and public gardens, make good plants for carpet bedding and knot gardens, but require constant trimming. Iresines will grow in an average potting mixture. Prune constantly to prevent leggy growth. If allowed to dry out, they wilt. Plants in sunny south windows require constant watering from February to May. Cuttings root easily in water. Take several in early spring for small plants to set out in the garden in spring, after all danger of frost is over. Use them freely in bare spots for touches of color all summer. Pot them in the fall, and bring indoors for the winter.

Bougainvillea

(Bougainvillea)

It is only within the last decade or so that this spectacular vine from Brazil has been grown as a house plant. Since it flowers when young, it makes a good one, whether trained on a lattice network, shaped into a tidy shrub, or placed in a hanging basket. What appear to be flowers are "bracts"—that is, colored leaves—surrounding small white true flowers in the centers.

Provide as much as sun as possible in winter for best performance. Not fussy about soil, bougainvillea tolerates wetness and dryness. Grow as cool as possible, and give an average soil mixture. Rest after flowering by gradually decreasing amount of watering. Hardwood cuttings root in sand and peat. Spring is the best time to propagate.

Bougainvillea, like poinsettia, is a short-day, long-night plant. If covered with a basket in the late afternoon during the late summer, so that day length is shortened, flowers appear around Christmas. Covering plants in fall results in early winter display. Ordinarily, bougainvillea is a winter-blooming vine, though its long-lasting bracts last into spring. Feed plants with liquid fertilizer as soon as color appears.

Magenta *Bougainvillea glabra* is the familiar flamboyant vine that clambers over rooftops and walls in gardens in the tropics. Its purple form, *B. g. sanderiana*, is very floriferous. *B. g. barrisi*, considered a variety, is grown for its small, variegated, creamy-white leaves. Other variations are Barbara Karst, deep red; Choisy, purple; and Miss Butt, scarlet-red. *B. spectabilis*, with large blunt-pointed leaves on very thorny stems, is a bright rose-red. Its form Crimson Lake is a more vibrant crimson. Other available varieties are California Gold and Texas Dawn, a newcomer described as Tyrian rose.

Calla Lily

(*Zantedeschia*)

Like amaryllis, calla lily, not a true lily, but a member of the arum family (first cousin of philodendron and Jack-in-the-pulpit), makes an easy pot plant. Unlike daffodils, tulips, and other Dutch bulbs, it does not require a cool rooting period, often difficult to achieve under average home conditions.

With its large, shiny, heart- or arrow-shaped leaves and bold flowers, comprised of a spathe and spadix on which the tiny true flowers are clustered, calla lily is a handsome plant, tropical in its appearance. It comes from South Africa, but can actually withstand considerable cold. In frost-free Ireland, it grows at doorways of thatch-roofed cottages.

Calla lily bulbs are usually potted in the fall, in September and October, for winter flowering. They can also be started in early spring

Spotted calla lily

for summer bloom. Either method gives good results, provided bulbs receive their normal resting period after flowering. Do not expect the same bulbs to perform twice without a rest. (In warm areas where they grow in the open ground, they often flower intermittently throughout the year.)

Bulbs can be started in small pots, to be shifted later, or in large five-, six-, or eight-inch pots, depending on variety. Cover with an inch of soil, but allow two inches of space at top of pot to fill in with more soil as shoot develops. Use an average potting mixture.

Water sparingly at first, but as plants grow, feed regularly (every two or three weeks) with liquid fertilizer as they are heavy feeders. They need sun and do best at cool temperatures, but they tolerate readings in the seventies. Gradually decrease watering after flowering, when leaves show indications of yellowing. Store in pots, and start again the following session. To make new plants, remove offsets or sow seeds, which take a few years to reach flowering size.

The common calla lily (*Zanthedeschia aethiopica*) grows over two feet tall and produces huge, leathery, creamy-white flowers with yellow spadixes; blooms last a long time. The smaller baby calla lily (*Z. a.*

minor) is recommended for window sill culture. Diminutive and freer flowering is the Godefrey calla lily (*Z. a. godefreyana*). Smaller than the common calla lily, only one and a half feet tall, is the spotted calla lily (*Z. albo-maculata*), with heavily white-spotted leaves and white, slender, trumpet flowers, purplish in center.

The golden calla lily (*Z. elliottiana*), nearly as large as the common calla, has ten-inch, light green leaves, spotted white. A vigorous grower, its funnel flowers are pure golden-yellow. Foliage is attractive when bulbs are not in bloom. About a foot tall, or somewhat higher, is the small pink calla lily (*Z. rehmanni*), with slender, arching, swordlike leaves, unlike those of the other callas. Flowers are pink, often touched with lavender-rose. It is excellent for a narrow window sill, where others are too large. Pink calla lily is also different because of its leaves. When not in bloom, it is difficult to recognize as calla.

Chinese Hibiscus

(Hibiscus rosa-sinensis)

Even those who have not visited the Hawaiian Islands are familiar with the flaming red hibiscus worn by native girls in their dark hair. Now that Americans are traveling widely, they know first-hand about this free-flowering shrub, encountering it in gardens in frost-free regions of the world.

Chinese hibiscus

Chinese hibiscus, also called Rose of China, is a large shrub (sometimes grown as a tree or standard), with three- to four-inch, shiny, dark green leaves, oval and tapering at the tips, and bright-red, hollyhock-like blossoms, accented with a long column on which pistils and stamens appear. Each blossom lasts two days; on the first it is fresh and crisp; on the second, it shows signs of wilting and browning along edges. Flowers may be single or double, sometimes fringed, but usually solitary. In addition to the fiery-red species, varieties span a wide range of colors—rose, pink, yellow, apricot, orange, and white.

As a house plant, Chinese hibiscus does best if given sun and kept cool. It usually flowers in winter. On the whole, it is undemanding, requiring ordinary care. Tree forms, or standards, can be used for accent, whether singly or in groupings. Plants will flower in summer or winter. If you prefer summer color, rest your plants in winter by giving little water and withholding fertilizer. For winter flowering, disbud in summer and give only a little or no food.

Prune and cut back in March, removing dead and weak wood and shaping to improve appearance. Feed or repot, if needed, using an average mixture. Softwood cuttings may be rooted in peatmoss and sand in spring; root hardwood cuttings in fall.

Striking varieties include Brilliant Queen, double scarlet; Orange Beauty; and Peachblow, double pink. *Hibiscus r. cooperi* is a dwarf, with narrow, variegated leaves and small, scarlet flowers. Chinese hibiscus blossoms are said to be used to dye hair. It is also used for blackening shoes, which is why it is called "shoeblack plant."

Crown-of-Thorns

(*Euphorbia splendens*)

With its thick, curving, prickly stems, crown-of-thorns is an old-timer that continues to hold a strong, impelling kind of fascination among gardeners.

Even if it tends to lose its small, blunt-tipped, light green leaves, it guarantees a year-round display of small, eye-catching, bright scarlet flowers. These appear mostly at the tips, and are actually composed of two bracts, resembling petals, on inch-long stems. Light green at first, they turn pinkish and later become fiery-red. This old and bizarre succulent is a first cousin of poinsettia. Both produce "flowers" made up of bracts; both give off a sticky, milky juice when cut.

As crown-of-thorns develops, its stems nearly become vining, form-ing interesting shapes as they intertwine to support one another. Since it requires considerable space, start to prune when small.

A native of Madagascar, crown-of-thorns needs the sunniest win-dow you have. The cheerful "flowers" appear primarily in winter. In fall, give plants less sun and keep soil somewhat dry in order to let the plant rest; flowering will then be more profuse. A light, sandy soil, as recommended for cacti, is suitable, but use room-temperature water, as chilling from cold water causes leaves and blossoms to drop.

You will have to accept one fact about crown-of-thorns: it always has yellow leaves. I have noticed this even on plants in Florida gardens. Apparently this is characteristic of the species, but it is not serious, since the spiny, snaky stems always retain their strange allure.

Always be sparing with water. Feed with light liquid fertilizer in January, February, and March, when plants flower freely. Avoid drafts and sudden drops in temperature, as either will cause leaves to turn yellow overnight. Cuttings root best in early spring or summer. First allow stems to dry for several hours in order to form calluses before inserting in moist sand or placing in water. Overwatering will cause rotting; rooting is slow, especially in winter.

Superior and generally more desirable is the dwarf crown-of-thorns (*E. S. bojeri*). Also native to Madagascar, it remains compact and sheds leaves less freely, becoming leggy only if neglected. Because of its more upright habit, it takes up less space. Crown-of-thorns is striking when grown in an earthenware pot or in a container glazed a vivid blue.

Donkey's Tail

(*Sedum morganianum*)

This succulent, with long trailing stems resembling chains, is an unusual plant, with a character all its own. Burro's tail is another name for this recent introduction, which was discovered in Coatepec, Mex-ico, in 1935. Its hanging stems, which arise from older branches close to the base, are clothed with short, thick, closely placed leaves that overlap, gray-green or silvery-green in color.

A slow grower, plants three to four feet long are estimated to be six to eight years old. Pink-red flowers appear at tips of mature specimens. With its heavy stems and strange leaf pattern, it then becomes an exotic sight.

Donkey's tail

Donkey's tail makes a superb hanging basket plant in a sunny window. Allow it plenty of space to show off its unique form to advantage. In southern California, where it is hardy outdoors, it is often seen atop stone walls, cascading like a small, pendulous vine.

The first time I grew this sedum, I found it easy, but found that it requires more water than other succulents. If allowed to dry out too much, the leaves shrivel and drop. Yet excessive moisture can be injurious. Plant in soil recommended for succulents.

Since the leaves of donkey's tail break off from their stems and drop if hit abruptly, keep plants where they are not apt to be brushed accidently. Leaves that drop will root in sand to make new plants. *Sedum morganianum* was named for Dr. Meredith Morgan of Richmond, California, the first person in this country to bring a plant into bloom. The flowers that appeared at the ends of three-foot-long stems were analyzed and placed in the crassula family.

Flowering Maple

(Abutilon)

So-called because its leaves resemble those of maple, flowering maple is a misnomer for this shrubby plant, which produces pendulous, papery, hollyhock-like flowers, and is related to hibiscus and the rose of Sharon. It was a featured plant in sunny windows several decades ago, and before central heating it grew with ease because it likes cool temperatures; if possible, grow at 60° F., with sun during the winter months.

Most plants available today are listed under *Abutilon hybridum*. Varieties come in an assortment of colors, including red, pink, orange, yellow, and white, with blossoms that appear intermittently throughout the year. For winter-flowering plants, take cuttings in early fall, even though they root more slowly than in spring. Seed sown in early spring will produce flowering plants for summer, for pot culture or to grow in the open ground.

Flowering maple

The chief drawback of flowering maple is its tendency to become leggy. To prevent this, pinch frequently, and prune in early spring and in early fall, when plants are ready to be taken indoors. This will promote a bushy habit, with several side branches that will carry the showy hanging blossoms. Except for this, culture is simple; plants wilt quickly if allowed to dry out.

Another tendency is that leaves are constantly turning yellow. There are some to pull off every day, but on healthy plants new ones replace the old regularly.

A smaller-leaved kind, *A. megapotamicum*, is outstanding in a hanging basket. Slender, gracefully drooping stems support small arrow-shaped leaves and yellow flowers, with long red calyxes, remindful of fuchsia. Delightful is the form *A. m. variegatum*, with strongly mottled yellow and green leaves and orange flowers. The foliage alone makes it a showy candidate for a bright window. When taken outdoors in summer, flowering maples require less sun, thriving well in partial shade. Feed regularly, indoors and out, to aid blooming.

Gardenia

(Gardenia jasminoides)

There are house plants that experience a rise and fall in popularity, like palms, rubber plants, and Boston ferns. One house plant that has maintained a steady appeal for decades is gardenia, even though it is a bit tricky.

Practically, everybody loves gardenia, a shrub with glossy, dark green leaves and waxy, creamy-white flowers that have a sweet but heady fragrance. As a flower for wedding bouquets and corsages, gardenia rates with the rose, orchid, carnation, and camellia.

In its native southern China, gardenia enjoys a warm, humid climate. It came to the western world by way of the Cape of Good Hope (hence one of its other common names, cape jasmine), and was named for Dr. Alexander Garden, an eighteenth-century physician and botanist who lived in Charleston, South Carolina. In the South, it is a common garden shrub.

To grow well, gardenia requires a high degree of humidity. Where mechanical humidifiers provide this, it grows with ease. Humidity can be increased by keeping the plant close to pans filled with water, by resting pots on a layer of moistened pebbles, and by mist spraying or bathing foliage once or twice a week.

Gardenia likes warmth with temperatures in the seventies during the day and a five degree drop at night; lower than 60° F. can be chilling. Like azalea and camellia, it is an acid-loving plant. Buy specially packaged acid soil or mix four parts good garden soil, three parts sand, three parts peatmoss, one part leafmold, and one-half part dry manure.

Give sun at east, south, or west exposures; if too hot in late winter, move to other windows or move back from the glass. Keep soil moist, but avoid overwatering, as this may cause buds and flowers to drop. Plants can be watered by placing their pots in a partly-filled basin of water until soil surface becomes moist.

In early spring, feed with a liquid fertilizer, 4-12-4 or 5-10-5, to aid new growth. Or use special acid fertilizers, also recommended for azalea and camellia. If foliage turns yellowish, as it often does, minor elements in the soil may be lacking. Micronized iron applied according to directions will restore coloring to anemic leaves.

Place plants outdoors in part shade when all danger of frost is over. Repot if needed, and prune to shape. Water and feed regularly all summer and bring indoors early, since foliage is susceptible to the lightest frost. But dropping may be due to over- or underwatering, sudden temperature changes, drafts, an alkaline soil, or a series of dull, cloudy days in winter, when it is advisable to give plants artificial lighting. Eliminate mealy bugs and scale with a soft brush dipped in wood alcohol or two to three sprayings with kelthane or a miticide.

Two kinds of gardenias are generally grown as house plants. One is the small-flowering *Gardenia jasminoides*, called cape jasmine in the South. Its natural flowering period is summer, when plants give their best performance, whether outdoors or in. The other, larger flowering, is the florist's or Veitchi type, which is inclined to flower in winter. Buds often drop during extended periods of cloudy weather. Remove buds in winter if you prefer bloom in summer.

Once special needs of gardenia are mastered, it is no more difficult or temperamental than other house plants.

Geranium

(*Pelargonium*)

On the whole, geraniums make good house plants, even if they do not bloom, growing best in temperatures in the fifties and low sixties. This condition does not exist in the average home; yet geraniums grow surprisingly well at higher readings, if given maximum sun and kept somewhat dry.

There are several ways to winter geraniums. One is to root cuttings in late summer or early fall for small-flowering plants for sunny window sills. With a sharp knife or scissors take cuttings, three to four inches long, from mature, hardened tips, with leaves spaced closely together. Stems with leaves spaced far apart are soft and apt to rot. Allow cuttings to dry out for several hours, and then strip off lower leaves, leaving two or three at the top. Also pull off the small wings along the stems, because they tend to encourage rotting.

Dip ends of cuttings in hydrated lime to insure a greater percentage of rooting, and insert lower half in pure sand or a 50-50 mixture of sand and peatmoss in flats, small pots, or bulb pans. Place in shade, water, and maintain even moisture thereafter—but not wetness. Cuttings will also root in water. Use opaque containers, which shut out light.

Transplant cuttings to individual two and one-half-inch pots when well rooted. First lift one or two to determine if roots have developed. For a potting mixture, use three parts light, sandy soil and one part peatmoss or leafmold, adding a teaspoon of bonemeal or superphosphate to a five-inch potful of soil.

After potting, place in strong light, and gradually move to sun as roots develop. By late September or October, depending on the weather, bring indoors to sunny windows. Later shift to three- and four-inch pots, using the same soil mixture. Pinch to keep bushy. In March or April, cut back hard to stimulate branching; in May, plant outdoors.

A second method is to retain the original plants. If in moderate-sized pots, cut back tops to six or eight inches just before bringing indoors. Place in sunny windows in the house or basement or other frost-free place.

Plants in the ground can be potted. Lift as carefully as possible since geraniums have few roots and soil is inclined to fall apart. Cut back, and place in sunny windows. They will shed many leaves, but they will recover for reuse in the garden in spring. Do the same with

Geraniums

variegated geraniums, much admired for their multicolored leaves. Among them are Miss Burdette Coutts, green, rosy-pink and creamy-white; Skies of Italy, crimson and yellow; Mrs. Cox, vermillion, purple and yellow. Leaf coloring is more intense in full sun.

Old-timers recall how it was possible to lift geraniums bare-rooted, and hang them upside down for the winter, in the "dirt" cellars of old houses. These cellars lacked furnaces, yet remained frost-free. In spring, the withered sticks were planted outdoors, where they developed into flowering plants. This, of course, is not possible in the hot, dry, insulated basements of today's houses. Those with cool cellars still succeed with this method.

Along with zonal and variegated geraniums, include some of the scented ones, which are prized for the delightful fragrance they give off when the leaves are crushed between fingertips—rose, lemon, nutmeg, cinnamon, peppermint, pine, ginger, orange, apple, balm, strawberry, and apricot. They are fun to collect, and easier to grow than zonals.

Grow a few dwarfs, which are classified according to size—small, medium, and large. Their names are beguiling—Sparkle, Goblin, Perky, Dopey, Pixie, Pigmy, Darling, Mischief, Frolic, Ruffles, Tweedle Dee and Tweedle Dum. Plant in three-inch pots. Do not overfeed, or they will outgrow their dwarfness.

All geraniums do best in full sun, preferably cool. Keep soil barely dry, and feed with high-phosphorous fertilizer in February and March to promote bloom. Pinch and prune regularly for bushy growth. The dwarfs are somewhat trickier than the larger kinds.

Otaheite Orange

(Citrus taitensis)

If there is a pot plant that evokes more admiration when in full fruit than this, it is hard to name, unless it is the similar Calamondin orange (*C. mitis*). Plants fresh from the florist at Christmas time are irresistibly beguiling when heavily laden with diminutive oranges. I prefer such a plant to poinsettia, cyclamen, or even azalea.

Otaheite orange has been a popular florist's plant for many years. Though its leaves will often drop because of insufficient light, too dry air, over- or underwatering, the colorful fruits, one and a half to two inches across, persist usually for several months. Blossoms appear with new growth in spring, while old fruits linger.

The more recent Calamondin orange, native to the Phillipines, is much grown in the Hawaiian Islands, where it is called "China orange." More upright in habit, fruits develop on erect clusters on branches that later bend over because of their weight. They are orange-yellow when ripe.

These two ornamental oranges are small shrubs, with dark green shiny leaves, pungent when crushed. Both these oranges are tricky because they need cool temperatures in winter, 45° to 60° F. Yet they fare well if kept warmer, if given sun, and if soil is kept moist but not wet. Plants resent drying out. If this happens a few times, leaves will shrivel in about ten days and then begin to drop, even before turning yellow. Suspend feeding in winter, but commence with light applications in early spring when new growth is on its way. If repotting, use a general mixture, with bonemeal or superphosphate added. Plants do best if slightly pot-bound.

With the new growth comes the small, waxy, short-lived, creamy-white flowers that have been immortalized by poets and lyricists for their exquisite and haunting fragrance. If plants are placed outdoors, bees will automatically take care of pollination. If indoors, shake vigorously so pollen will drop from one blossom to another. Or transfer pollen with a small soft brush or your fingertips. Plants summering in the garden or terrace should be brought indoors early to adjust to their new enviroment before central heating is turned on. Scale and mealy bugs, common pests, can be controlled with malathion.

Fruits of the ornamental oranges are not edible, but their juice can be used, like lemons and limes, to flavor cool summer drinks.

Other kinds of citrus plants grown as pot plants require similar care. One of the most appealing is Meyer lemon, discovered by the plant explorer, Frank N. Meyer, in China. Small-growing, dense-foliaged when healthy, its fruits, which appear even on small plants, are large, thin-skinned, and very juicy. Huge are the fruits of the dwarf Ponderosa lemon, with larger leaves than those of Otaheite orange. It is not unusual for flowers and fruits to appear on plants at the same time.

If you want to try the lesser known kumquats, three dwarf kinds are recommended: Nagami, Meiwa, and Marumi. Technically, they are not citrus plants, for they belong to the genus *Fortunella*, though the family, *Rutaceae*, is the same. Culture is similar.

Kumquat fruits, oval in shape and an inch in diameter, are bright orange in color. They can be eaten wholly, including the rind, which is thick and sweeter than the acid-tasting flesh. The peel makes excellent marmalade.

Oxalis

(*Oxalis*)

These are delightful sun-loving plants, with three-part clover-like leaves that fold downward at night, and tiny tubular flowers that close with darkness. Two types are grown as house plants: fibrous-rooted, which grow all year round, and bulbous (or semi-bulbous), which rest after flowering.

The most common is the old-fashioned window-box oxalis (*Oxalis rubra*), with rosy-lavender flowers, classified as semi-bulbous; it can be grown all year or rested. I rest mine by withholding water in spring and start the bulbs again in the fall. One I watered October 1st began to flower on October 23rd. Remove yellow leaves and old flowers by tugging abruptly with the thumb and forefinger. Also semi-bulbous is the compact white *O. regnelli.*

There are several bulbous kinds of oxalis. *O. bowieana* has large leaves and pink flowers, nearly two inches across, which appear all winter. Most vigorous is the yellow Bermuda buttercup (*O. cernua*) from South Africa, which has naturalized in Bermuda and Florida; it has a double form. The lavender *O. incarnata* is a fast grower, and the bright rose *O. hirta* has hairy, leathery leaves. Plants first grow erect, then bend over before starting to trail.

O. carnosa, a native of Chile, belongs to the fibrous-rooted group. It has yellow flowers, thick stems and succulent leaves. Oxalis Grand Duchess (*O. variabilis*) from the Cape of Good Hope has large flowers that may be pink, violet, or white. I find that leaves usually turn yellow in prolonged cloudy weather. Cut these with scissors, but do not pull. The fibrous, upright fishtail oxalis (*O. ortgiesi*) has notched dark green leaves, reddish beneath, which close at night or in dark weather. Tiny yellow flowers unfold almost constantly.

Oxalis do best if grown around 60° - 65° F. They make excellent window sill plants, where they enjoy cool air at night. Use average potting mixture, with extra sand or vermiculite added, plus a sprinkling of lime. Keep moist, since roots do not like to dry out; soggy soil is harmful. Aid flowering with light applications of liquid fertilizer. On the whole, oxalis are among the few flowering house plants that are easy.

Poinsettia

(*Euphorbia pulcherrima*)

This flamboyant native of Mexico was named for Dr. Joel R. Poinsett, United States Minister to Mexico, who brought it to this country in 1828. Today it flourishes in gardens in warm regions throughout the world. A member of the spurge family, it is closely related to the crown-of-thorns. Poinsettia's "flower" petals are actually colored leaves known as bracts, whose function is to attract insects to the small, yellow, inconspicuous true flowers, which appear in the centers.

A charming legend tells the story of the origin of poinsettia: Many Christmases ago, there was a little Mexican girl named Pepita, who was very sad because she did not possess pesos to buy the Infant Jesus a gift. Walking sorrowfully to church with her cousin, Pedro, she told him her secret. Though proud of the candle he held for the Infant, Pedro tried to console his unhappy companion. "The Infant Jesus will like any kind of gift, no matter how small, if it is given in love," he assured her. This cheered little Pepita, who stopped and gathered some weeds that grew by the roadside. Yet, she remained doubtful, and remarked: "I have plenty of love, Pedro, but these weeds. . . ."

When Pepita walked into the church, the light from the Child was so blinding, she forgot all embarrassment about her gift, and quickly placed it at His feet. As she stepped back, she noticed that her weeds had turned into beautiful, flaming red flowers. "Flor de Noche Buena" —"Flower of Holy Night"—everyone called these gorgeous blossoms, which the little Mexican offered with all her love.

Poinsettia is not an easy house plant. Of tropical origin, it is sensitive to temperature changes. Florist plants brought into the house often lose their lower leaves, and not for reasons of neglect. This occurs because plants, which come from the coddled atmosphere of the greenhouse, are suddenly transferred to darkened flower markets and florist shops, where cold blasts of air strike them when doors are opened.

Give poinsettia a warm, sunny window, free from drafts. Keep moist at all times, and spray with a mist atomizer. For a more graceful appearance, remove some of the stiff stakes inserted by growers to make shipment easier. With basic care, plants should keep well for a month or more.

New varieties tend to hold their bracts, and growers also apply a hormone spray to make the bracts last longer. Leaves usually drop first, leaving bare stems with a few bracts at the tops.

Despite this delicate facet, poinsettia is a really tough plant. When abandoned for weeks and months, it goes dormant, but springs to life again when watered. This rest period is part of the growth cycle. When the last bracts have fallen in late January, February, or March, let up on watering gradually and store plants in the basement, an unused room, a closet, or other storage place, with temperatures above freezing; water it occasionally.

With warm spring weather, cut the stems back to four to six inches. Repot or, if you prefer, remove an inch or two of soil from the surface and add a fresh mixture. Water well, and relegate to a sheltered spot outdoors, such as a porch or terrace. Or insert the pot up to its rim in open ground. Water and feed it all summer long, when new growth will be vigorous.

Poinsettia tends to become leggy, but this is to be expected from a woody shrub that grows over ten feet tall. Prune the plant by cutting the new shoots back to four leaves when about eight leaves have developed. Repeat this process during the summer, but stop pruning around Labor Day in order to insure blooms by Christmas.

41

New plants can be started from cuttings. These will give you shorter, less leggy plants. Start in July and early August to take four- to six-inch cuttings. Use a sharp knife, and cut straight rather than at a slant, just below the node or leaf bud. Cuttings will bleed less if taken with a heel—that is, with a piece of stem. To prevent wilting in hot weather, immerse cuttings in cold water immediately, and plant in moist sand as soon as possible. Dip ends in a hormone powder to hasten rooting. To provide humidity, root in an old aquarium or in a small propagating kit covered with a plastic frame.

Plant cuttings in soil as soon as roots appear, as stems tend to lose their lower leaves if left in the sand too long. Use any good potting mixture, with sand added, and at first shade the young plants from hot sun, but give them good light. By late August or early September transfer them to flowering-sized pots, using rich soil—four parts loam, one-half part sand, one-half dry manure, plus a sprinkling of bone-meal. If tips are pinched to keep plants shorter, blooms will be smaller. Poinsettia is sensitive to cold air and light frosts, so bring them indoors early—not later than Labor Day in the North. This also gives the plants an opportunity to adjust to the drier indoor air. Open windows on warm fall days.

Like chrysanthemum and Christmas cactus, poinsettia is a short-day, long-night plant, which waits for short days of winter to set flower buds. Keep plants away from artificial light at night. Place them in a warm room with no lights or cover with inverted cardboard boxes or baskets from 5 P.M. to 8 A.M. Discontinue this by mid-November, when flower buds show, continuing to avoid too much night light thereafter. Plants in commercial greenhouses near street lamps invariably show inferior bloom, so sensitive are poinsettias to light.

The person who is seriously interested in flowering a few plants of poinsettias indoors, or who is a collector and maintains a special room for this Christmas flower, will want to make a study of named varieties. The low-growing Barbara Ecke Supreme, with broad red bracts, is one of the best. Albert Ecke is a medium variety with large red bracts. Indianapolis Red, a short salmon-orange-red, pinches well and blooms later than others.

The medium variety Pink, with narrow rosy-pink bracts, is early, as is Ecke Pink, which propagates easily and pinches well. Spring Pink is late, remaining in good condition long after Christmas and into spring.

The medium Ecke White flowers early and lasts long, while Ecke White Supreme is similar except for its wider bracts. The red Henrietta Ecke is considered the best double.

Shrimp Plant

(Beloperone guttata)

If you have a sunny window and are eager for touches of winter color, grow shrimp plant, an attractive shrub that is appropriately named. Growing about two feet tall, its chief charm is its shrimp-like "flowers," which are made up of tiny white blossoms and colorful, long-lasting, reddish bracts. Overall effect is one of showy curving spikes, over three inches long, that unfold profusely on large, healthy plants.

The simple, oval, light leaves of shrimp plant, two and half inches long, appear on thin, wiry stems. Do not allow plants to dry out, as leaves wilt, often turning yellow and dropping later. This native of Mexico has the annoying tendency of becoming leggy. One way to avoid this is to grow plants in full sun in winter, which is needed for flowering and compact growth. Another is to pinch tips regularly and a third is to prune plants hard in early spring, before new growth starts, and again in the fall. Repot in spring and place outdoors in part sun; feed regularly with weak liquid fertilizer.

Bring indoors early, before the first frost and central heating is turned on. Some lower leaves will drop, but after a while this will cease. Best temperature is 55° to 65° F. but plants grow well under higher readings if not allowed to dry out. Shrimp plant thrives in an average potting mixture. Root cuttings, taken from the half-ripened shoots, for a supply of new plants to replace the old. A new and unusual form, with yellow bracts, is Yellow Queen.

Swedish Myrtle

(Myrtus communis)

I am very fond of this dainty, glossy-leaved shrub, if only because it is the true myrtle of the ancient Greeks. In Greece I have seen it in the wild and in the Garden of Hephaistos at the Theseum in Athens. The tiny, dark green leaves of this evergreen, which can be pruned and clipped like boxwood, are pleasantly aromatic when crushed between the fingers or rubbed in the palms of the hands. About an inch long,

43

they form the background for small white flowers that are followed by blue-black fruits.

Not native to Sweden, but rather to the Mediterranean, this plant is considered a necessary part of the trousseau of Swedish as well as German brides. This tradition apparently has its roots in antiquity, since the plant was associated with the goddess Aphrodite and was used at weddings in ancient Greece.

Swedish myrtle does best in a cool, sunny window. It can be grown at warmer temperatures, provided it has sunshine. Give an ordinary soil mixture, and keep moist. I find that it resents drying out, and this is somewhat surprising, because in its native Mediterranean areas it survives hot, dry summers. But in its native habitat roots reach deeply into the ground while, in confined pots, they are restricted.

Given a large pot and sufficient space, Swedish myrtle will develop into a handsome shrub. The form *M. c. compacta* is dwarf and dense; *M. c. nana* has tiny leaves. There are also variegated forms, the rare *M. c. variegata*, and the green and white *M. c. microphylla variegata*.

Swedish myrtle makes a thick, formal hedge, as seen in southern California and in the Alhambra Gardens at Granada, Spain. If you have several large plants in a cool room, remember to cut snippets to use in finger bowls. The "clean" scent of the crushed leaves is always refreshing.

Herbs for Kitchen Windows

There is nothing new about growing house plants in kitchen windows. For centuries, kitchens have been prime gathering places for family and friends, and it is only natural that plants should be grown there. In fact, you can hardly step into any kitchen without spotting some form of plant life: a garden rose given by a friend, a few sprigs of mint, a pot of chives, or African violet leaves or geranium cuttings rooting in water. Kitchen window sills and shelves act as a repository, where a miscellany of pots, jars, and cans with bits of plant life are kept for reasons of convenience. The kitchen, too, is usually the workshop where house plants are repotted, washed, and sprayed.

Plants generally do well in kitchens. Less apt to be neglected, they also benefit from humidity from the washing of dishes and clothes. Where cooking gas is no problem, everything else favors kitchens as ideal places for pot plants. If they are elegant, use plants as decoration, and avoid the clutter of odds and ends that is often found in old-time kitchens.

No hard and fast rules dictate what to grow in kitchens; select plants

Kitchen herbs: catnip, hyssop, salad burnet, and costmary.

according to preference and amounts of light, including exposure to direct sunlight. With higher humidity, especially at windows close to the sink, it is possible to grow many kinds of plants such as episcias, gloxinias, and other gesneriads, fittonias, pellionias, crossandras, aphelandras, and ferns. Kitchens are often associated with abundant, bright sunshine; "sunny kitchen windows" is a common phrase. This largely goes back to old-fashioned kitchens, which were purposely located on the south, east, or west sides of the house.

If kitchen windows are sunny, use them for flowering or bright-foliaged plants to add color. Sunshine radiates around the blossoms of geranium, azalea, shrimp plant, chrysanthemum, poinsettia, kalanchoe, tender narcissus, and Dutch bulbs. It intensifies the coloring of the foliage of coleus, velvet plant (*Gynura*), variegated geraniums, and blood-leaf (*Iresine*). Colorful curtains and gaily painted walls add cheer, even on dull, cloudy days. Hanging basket plants flourish if light is good—among them English, Swedish, or grape ivies, pothos, philodendrons, zebrinas, episcias, columneas (red-flowering *C. hirta* is a beauty), *Begonia rich*-mondensis; coleus Trailing Queen; or blue browallia.

45

Sunny kitchen windows are ideal for herbs. They are ornamental plants, and also snippets can be taken from them all winter long to flavor food. In summer, potted herbs can be kept outside by the door nearest the kitchen, where they are handy to snip for cooking.

Herbs are plants steeped in romance and lore, and for centuries it was hardly possible to preserve foods and to cure the sick without them. They also played significant roles in ceremonies pertaining to birth and death.

Herbs are divided into two groups: annual and perennial, and both kinds can be grown indoors. Annuals that can be started from seed include basil, dill, coriander, anise, fennel, borage, summer savory, sweet marjoram, and chervil. Dependable perennial types for indoors are apple, pineapple, and orange mints, oregano, rosemary, thymes, chives, parsley (biennial), spearmint, winter savory, sage, lemon balm, tarragon, and lemon verbena.

Culture is similar for the two groups. In the garden, herbs do best in lean soils; heavy soils, high in fertilizer, induce lush leaves, with less aroma and flavor. When growing herbs in pots, soil can be richer than in the garden because of limited root run. Use any good garden soil with fertilizer added, and include sand or perlite to lighten the mixture and aid drainage. Or you can mix three parts loam, one part sand, one part compost, with a sprinkling of dry manure, bonemeal, and lime rubble. For herbs, I prefer clay and earthenware pots to the plastic ones because of their natural appearance. They also dry out faster, which is an advantage since herbs particularly resent wetness. Four-inch pots are a convenient size, but several plants can be grown together in larger bulb pans or other containers.

Combine herbs with other house plants, unless you are a purist, but this is a matter of taste. Give routine care: water when soil is barely dry, spray foliage to freshen it, remove yellow leaves, and feed in late winter and early spring. If possible grow herbs where it is cool. In late spring, potted herbs, particularly perennial types, can be planted in the garden or transferred to larger containers and placed on porches, terraces, or back steps. In summer, sow seed of annual herbs to grow indoors in winter. In fall, lift thrifty specimens from the garden or take side shoots from mother plants.

Using herbs in cooking is a study in itself, one that is usually pursued by the culinary artist and the gourmet. The idea is to use just the right amounts with the right kinds of foods to improve and bring out flavor, since correctly seasoned foods stimulate appetite, aid digestion, and add the element of fragrance. Rosemary, for example, is recommended for chicken, veal, and fish, as well as lamb stew. Basil (curly and purple-leaved kinds) improves the flavor of fish, tomatoes, and salads. Mints, among the most versatile of herbs, do wonders for potato salad, peas, carrots, lamb, and jellies. Use tarragon in fish, and sprinkle oregano (also spelled origanum) on salads, pork, and vinegar. The tips of chive leaves will add mild onion flavor to omelets, salads, potatoes, soups, and cottage cheese. Use thyme in fish, meats, and poultry; put parsley in potato salad, soups, and tossed salads. And do not overlook dill for vinegar, pickles, and soups; its seeds are distinctive in pastries and cakes.

Fantastic Cacti and Succulents

Cacti and succulents comprise a fantastic, sometimes bizarre but fascinating, group of house plants. Either you like them or you do not. There hardly seems to be an in-between. As a group, cacti and succulents, which require the same care, are grown more for their forms than their blossoms. Theirs is a strange appeal. With their numerous thorns and spines, they are formidable and treacherous looking.

For contemporary interiors, cacti and succulents have a magic touch, with their geometric forms—some cylindrical or globular, others conical or linear—on which lovely blossoms appear. Many have appealing common names—old man, old lady, barrel, golden lace, golden ball, and barrel cactus.

Anyone can grow cacti and succulents. They are plants with fleshy and juicy stems that have the capacity to retain moisture for long periods of time. Native to desert regions, they survive on small amounts of water and tolerate hot, dry air.

Sunshine they do need; they like south, east, or west windows. In north exposures, they will live for incredibly long periods of time, but eventually will grow spindly. Often placed on glass shelves in sunny windows, they can be combined with other house plants for dramatic effects.

The cactus family is a large and widely diversified group. Native to the New World, some are tall and tree-like, as much as sixty feet high; others, low and squat, spread widely. Perhaps the most familiar of all of the cactus family are the Christmas cactus and the orchid cactus, also known as epiphyllum. Some of the more interesting kinds to try include the Old Lady Cactus (*Mammillaria bahniana*), a small grower with cylindrical stems covered with white bristles to 1½ inches long and pink blossoms; the Old Man Cactus (*Cephalocereus senilis*), a slow grower with round stems covered with white hairs and rose blooms up to two two-and-one-half inches across; and the common crimson-flowering Rat-tail Cactus (*Aporocactus flagelliformis*) with long trailing stems a half inch in diameter that are covered with bristly hairs. It can be trained to a support or grown in a hanging basket.

Others with appealing names include Silver Torch (*Cleistocactus straussi*), a handsome red-violet flowering species from Bolivia with light green stems up to three feet that are covered with white spines, and the Silver Ball Cactus (*Notocactus scopa*), a foot-tall globular type that is protected with white bristles and is especially attractive when the two-and-a-half-inch blossoms open.

Since cacti require minimum care, you may like to grow the Golden Barrel Cactus (*Ferocactus grusoni*), with light green stems covered with golden spines and yellow flowers that are brown on the outside. Grizzly Bear Opuntia (*Opuntia erinacea*), native to our Southwest, has erect branches that grow about a foot and a half tall and display formidable bristles. Red-yellow blooms measure two and a half inches across.

The list goes on and on to include peanut, organ pipe, pin-cushion, sea urchin, chin, snowball, hedgehog, cob, and sand dollar, all delightful names. Give cacti sun, minimum watering, feeding only during periods of growth, and repotting when needed.

As a group, succulents are more popular—sedum, echeveria, kalanchoe, aloe, crassula, crown-of-thorns, agave, and mesembryanthemum are familiar; less so are haworthia, kleinia, gasteria, stapelia, and huernia. Like cacti, they are grown more for interest than beauty.

Children delight in *Kalanchoe daigremontiana* because of the tiny plantlets along the thick, glaucous leaves, which drop to make new plants. More familiar is *K. blossfeldiana* and its forms, offered by florists as a Christmas plant, with clusters of tiny red flowers that last several weeks. Among aloes, *A. brevifolia*, from South Africa, is worthwhile. It has thorny teeth along the edges of thick, pointed leaves. *A. arborescens*, which attains several feet, has long arching, toothed leaves. Few plants are easier to grow; keep older stems cut for compact growth.

Give succulents sunshine. They tolerate warm or cool temperatures. Provide a well-drained soil; roots cannot stand wetness. A good mixture comprises one-half good garden loam and one-half coarse sand, with a sprinkling of well-decayed leafmold and agricultural lime. Yet another: two parts clean sand, one part garden loam, one part peatmoss, plus a scattering of charcoal and bonemeal.

Slow-growing plants can remain in the same pots for two or three years. Avoid overpotting; when time to repot, shift in late winter or early spring, after the dormant period, using pots next in size, but no larger. For those with spines and thorns, repotting is a ticklish operation. Use leather gloves and tongs to lift plants and hold them in position. Work with soil that is moist; after potting, plants will not require watering for a week or so until roots recover. Thereafter, water lightly twice a week for two weeks.

In the matter of watering, few plants are more misunderstood than cacti and succulents. Coming from desert and arid regions, they rot easily. In winter, from November to March, when days are short and often sunless, water once every week or two, preferably on sunny days so soil will dry out quickly. During the growing period, plants demand more moisture—as a thorough watering twice a week. Feed with a mixed food—5-10-5 or 5-8-7—but avoid overfeeding; these are slow growers and are unable to absorb excess amounts of food. Sprinkle and dig bonemeal or superphosphate into the surface of the soil in spring.

Place outdoors in warm weather, but protect from hot sun for a few days even if grown in full sun indoors. This will enable the "leaves," which are truly stems, to adjust gradually. Bring indoors before the first frost. On the whole, cacti and succulents have few problems. If overwatering causes rotting, discard plants. Scale and mealy bugs can be checked with malathion, but use kelthane for red spider mites.

(3)

Windows on the West

Western exposure is often compared to eastern. Though in opposite directions, both receive about the same amounts of sunshine. Western sun, like southern, is hot. It is already hot when it starts to creep into windows shortly after noon; it becomes hotter and hotter until it finally starts to cool off in the late afternoon.

That is the major difference between west and east. Morning sun increases in warmth and intensity as it rises in the sky; by the time it is high in the sky, it has moved around to the south and has disappeared from east-facing windows. Afternoon sun keeps growing hotter, but by the time it is low in the sky, when it reaches far into rooms, it has cooled off considerably. Both west and south windows are recommended for geraniums, cacti, succulents, and other sun-loving plants.

Each exposure has its special charm. The sun that disappears in the western sky often brings glorious sunsets. These are a source of great pleasure, and we enjoy them more than sunrises simply because we are up and about. In hot summer weather, the west has another charm. As the sun sets, the days cool off, and this brings much-needed relief. Afternoon sun is brighter and harsher than morning, which is soft and more luminous. Even noonday sun is less brittle, less saturating than western sun. As the afternoon advances toward sunset time, sunlight becomes softer.

As with other exposures, buildings and trees affect the sunshine at western windows. My study has three windows that face due west. For years I have grown Swedish ivy in a hanging basket. With a forty-foot elm tree fifteen feet away from the window. In winter, when the sun is weak, I often draw the Venetian blinds, in order to work at my desk. But in summer the elm shades my window, and I leave the blinds up. The winter growth of the Swedish ivy is sturdier than in summer, when ordinarily in a well-lit window the opposite would be true.

The following plants grow well in a western exposure.

Amaryllis

(Hippeastrum, also Amaryllis)

Do you know the charming legend of the amaryllis? Amaryllis was a beautiful maiden. Alteo, a handsome youth, was much sought after by all the maidens, but since he was more interested in his pursuit of horticulture, he rejected their advances with the reply: "Bring me a new flower, and my love shall be yours," Amaryllis sought the advice of the Delphic oracle, and the next evening, she pierced her heart with a golden arrow, and ran bare-footed to Alteo, shedding blood as she hastened. She repeated this several nights, until one evening her feet brushed bright crimson-red flowers along the path. Gathering these in armfuls, she sped to Alteo's hut, and when he saw the beautiful flowers, he succumbed immediately to the charms of Amaryllis.

Amaryllis is perhaps the easiest of bulbs to grow as a house plant. Newly purchased bulbs contain embryonic flower buds, and need only warmth, moisture, and light to grow. Like paper-white narcissus, they grow in water in pebbles or fibre.

This tender bulb, native to South Africa, is admired for its huge lily-like blossoms in startling reds and scarlets, pink and rose, orange, lavender, and pure white. Blooms appear at the top of a stem, usually when plants have not developed their leaves. Occasionally, flower stems come after leaves have grown, but this is less common. New amaryllis bulbs are sold during the fall and winter months. The Dutch hybrid strains are gorgeous and expensive, but are long-lived, flowering year after year with good care.

Give amaryllis an average potting mixture. It flowers best when pot-bound, so select a container that allows no more than an inch of space between the bulb and the sides. Place so that one-half or two-thirds of the top of the bulb protrudes from the soil. Add plenty of drainage material at the bottom, firm the soil, and water; then wait for flower shoot to appear. Bulbs need little water until growth starts.

Keep turning the pot around, and stake the flower stem if it is

51

Amaryllis

needed to prevent it from falling over with the weight of the blossoms. After flowering, cut stem to the base, but continue to water and feed plant to support the leaf growth, since healthy foliage insures bloom for the following year. In summer place pots outdoors in partial shade, water them, feed, and give the same care as other house plants. Bring indoors before the first frost, and start to withhold water for leaves to yellow and ripen. Start bulbs into growth again in early winter. By regulating temperature and the forcing period, plants may be brought into bloom for Christmas, New Year's, Valentine's Day, or even Easter.

Some gardeners prefer to set amaryllis bulbs in the open ground, where they need very little care all summer. In early fall lift the bulbs and store them at 65° to 70°F. Cut off the leaves when they turn brown, but do not remove the roots attached to the bulbs, as they are needed for good flowering. Rest bulbs about six weeks before potting for winter bloom.

Asparagus Fern

(Asparagus plumosus)

You doubtless know this plant, if only because you have seen it as "greens" in florist bouquets. Not a fern at all, it is a true asparagus; small spears that spring from the roots resemble miniature asparagus tips. These develop into a cloud of very fine, fern-like, dark green needles, only one-fourth-inch long. Wiry stems eventually grow several feet high; small white flowers are followed by black berries. Commonly grown as house plants are the dwarf forms, *A. p. compactus* and *A. p. nanus.*

Also feathery and fern-like is Sprenger asparagus (*A. sprengeri*), with slender, light green needles, three-fourths an inch long, on arching stems, ideal for hanging baskets. Like asparagus fern, it comes from South Africa; both are members of the lily family.

Small, fragrant whitish-pink flowers are followed by attractive red fruits. This vining plant is frequently used in window boxes in Europe, where it thrives equally well in full sun or shade. It is a popular ground cover in southern Europe, where it is hardy. Available are the dwarf *A. s. compactus* and the variegated *A. s. variegatus* forms.

Both these asparagus grow in ordinary soil, with sun for part of the day, preferably in a cool room. Keep the plant moist but not wet, and feed it in spring and summer. Sprenger asparagus does better in a dry atmosphere, but both tend to shed their leaves if old stems are not cut back to the base. Divide overgrown plants in early spring.

With its airy foliage, Sprenger asparagus makes an excellent trailing plant in window boxes. Use it as a substitute for the common variegated vinca. Plants can be wintered indoors, and separated in the very early spring for a plentiful supply. Also use it freely in hanging baskets outdoors in sun or shade.

Avocado

(Persea americana)

Alligator pear is another common name for this tropical tree. It may be started from the pits of the fruits, saved when the flesh is used for salads. To root the large, hard seed from this green, pear-shaped fruit and watch its strong spike shoot upward and break into leaf is fascinating.

The name "pear" refers to the similarity of shape to the common eating fruit, but according to Curtis's Botanical Magazine (1851), "alligator" is perhaps "a corruption of Aguacate, one of the names by which . . . it is known in Lima (Peru)."

In its native American habitats avocado attains sixty feet. As a house plant it is shorter, grown for its large, elongated, ovalish leaves. They are like those of common rubber plant, except smaller—four to eight inches long. Fruit, however, cannot be expected, though in conservatories large plants produce small greenish flowers at tips of the branches.

Avocado seed can be rooted in water, soil, or peatmoss and sand. For children it is more exciting to start it in a glass of water, so they can watch through the sides as the roots develop. First soak the seed in water for a few days to remove the outer covering, if it does not come off easily. Insert three toothpicks or wooden match sticks at equidistant points into the sides of the seed, and suspend the seed on the toothpicks on the rim of a glass, adding enough water to cover the bottom half of the seed. If the pit should rot, it is due to disease spores. Rooting it in moist peatmoss and sand or in light soil is usually safer.

Roots sometimes take several weeks to develop. When they appear, along with a shoot, plant the pit in a general potting mixture, with enough crocks at the bottom of the pot for good drainage. Place the top of the seed about a half inch below the surface of the soil. Start with a small pot, shifting to a larger size as the plant develops. If you prefer, plants can be left to grow in water for several months—or long as two years.

Growth will be fast, but this is not surprising as this is a forest tree. Keep transferring the plant into larger pots until eventually you pot it in a tub. Avocado is a heavy feeder: be generous with feeding during growing period. Watering is tricky. Insufficient amounts cause leaves to wilt and feel like paper to the touch. They revive with watering but edges later turn brown. Overwatering rots the thick, fleshy roots, especially during the rest period.

The biggest problem is what to do with an alligator pear plant when it reaches the ceiling. Prune it hard frequently; cut back shoots to the last cluster of leaves before new growth starts. Plants can be grown as shrubs or trained as a tree with a single trunk by removing side branches on young specimens to the desired point. Place plants outdoors in partial shade in summer, but bring indoors early, as the large leaves are sensitive to frosts.

Camellia

(*Camellia*)

Few shrubby flowering evergreen plants have more admirers than camellia. In the South, it is one of the most prized garden plants. In the North, where its flowers are a florist's winter-time specialty, it has a large following among indoor gardeners, especially those with cool home greenhouses.

Camellia is one plant that has everything except fragrance. Its lovely blossoms, single or double, which come in a wide range of colors that run through the reds, pinks, and whites, are so perfectly formed that they look unreal. Very dark green leaves, highly polished, make plants attractive all year round.

Camellia

The clue to the success in growing camellia in winter is cool temperatures. A range between 40° and 55° F is best, though daytime readings can be higher if they are followed by a drop at night.

Camellias are often grown in unheated rooms or in breezeways or other enclosures, including sun-heated winter pits, where temperatures stay above freezing. On very cold nights, plants can be moved elsewhere to a warmer spot until arctic weather passes.

Like azalea and gardenia, camellia is an acid-loving plant. It needs a soil rich in organic matter: one part soil, one part leafmold or peatmoss, and one-half part dehydrated manure. You can buy special acid soil at a garden center.

Keep soil constantly moist, especially during the flowering period and in spring and summer, when growth is active. If pot-bound, shift to larger containers in early spring. In time, plants will require tubs or very large plastic or clay pots. Place outdoors in summer in partial shade. Be generous with watering and feeding, using an acid fertilizer. Syringe the foliage regularly, and bring indoors before first frost, after cleaning and spraying with malathion to rid the plant of possible mealy bugs, scale, and aphids.

From October to April, the flowering period, bud droping is a common problem. It is usually caused by insufficient sunshine, too high temperatures, particularly at night, over- or underwatering, or dry air. Syringe foliage often, taking plants, if small, to the bathtub for a shower.

Flower buds are formed with the new growth during the summer months. Prune plants after flowering in late winter or in early spring. Among popular varieties for indoor culture are Debutante, double pink; Alba-plena, double white; and Chandleri Elegans, semi-double rose and white.

Christmas Cactus

(Zygocactus truncatus)

This is one of the most widely grown house plants. When its arching stems (they resemble leaves) are covered with pendulous, rose-pink, lantern-like blossoms, the plants become indescribably beautiful, a transformation that is sudden. Flowers appear over a long period during the season of short, dull days.

Christmas cactus is unusually long-lived, often becoming an heirloom, like camellia, agapanthus, oleander, clivia, and sweet bay. A letter from Mrs. William G. Coburn, Pemaquid Harbor, Maine, relates a typical experience with this old-time plant. She writes: "My Christmas cactus was brought here by my mother-in-law as a bride in 1893. She lived with me the last fifteen years of her life, and the plant became mine in December, 1961. In the winter of 1964–65 it produced 185 blossoms, and 191 in 1965–66. For years it has been in a ten-inch pot and has a spread of thirty-six inches. It has not been repotted for at least ten years. It usually starts flowering at the end of November, takes a couple of weeks' rest in February, and then continues to bloom into March."

The clue to success with Christmas cactus is neglect. Coming from the mountain forests of Brazil, like many orchids and bromeliads, it grows in organic matter in the crotches of trees, where it receives filtered sunshine and undergoes annually a rainy and dry season. After the wet period, plants go dormant, but then retain sufficient moisture in their succulent leaves to survive.

To insure bloom, reduce watering gradually in early October until the soil is quite dry, allowing the plant to rest for six to eight weeks. Keep it in a cool, sunny window at 50° to 60° F., and make sure it does not receive artificial illumination at night. Christmas cactus is a short-day, long-night plant. It sets flowers buds when nights become long.

When buds appear at the tips, give plants more sun and water and apply mild liquid fertilizer until the flowers open. Too much feeding and high temperatures cause bud dropping. After the blooms have faded, rest the plant again for five to six weeks. Then resume watering and feeding for the new spring growth.

Christmas cactus flowers best when it is pot bound. Feed established plants with bonemeal and mixed fertilizer annually. When ready to repot, shift plants in early spring, using a soil of equal parts good loam, sand, peatmoss or leafmold, plus a teaspoon of a 4-12-4 or 5-10-5 fertilizer to a six-inch pot. Add some broken charcoal to provide good drainage. Cuttings taken when plants are inactive root easily in moist sand or loose compost. Control mealy bugs and scale with malathion or with a soft brush dipped in wood alcohol.

Few indoor gardeners know that Christmas cactus produces showy, purplish-red fruits, which remain decorative for as long as two years. To produce fruit, transfer pollen from one flower to another with a soft brush, using blossoms from entirely different plants (not even cuttings from the mother plant) or from the two species of Christmas cactus that are commonly grown indoors.

The so-called true Christmas cactus (*Zygocactus truncatus*) has sharp teeth along the stems, and is sometimes called crab cactus. It flowers from October until January.

A closely related plant, also commonly refereed to as Christmas cactus, is actually Bridge's cactus (*Schlumbergera bridgesi*), and has no teeth along the margins. It flowers from November until February. Culture is the same for both. Actually the nomenclature of Christmas cactus remains confusing.

Chrysanthemum

(*Chrysanthemum*)

I am often asked if florist chrysanthemum pot plants will flower again and if they are hardy enough to plant in the garden. Most varieties grown in pots are not hardy outdoors in colder regions of the country, including metropolitan areas of Boston, New York, Chicago, and Detroit. They survive winters if given good protection or if placed in a coldframe. In warmer parts of the country, where there is freezing, florist chrysanthemums are hardy, and will flower year after year if given routine care.

To raise in pots, growers select varieties that are especially showy and produce large blooms. These often include such exotic types as spider, cascade, anemone, and spoon. The person who has the time and inclination can bring old plants into bloom again. A friend who maintains that she "knows nothing about house plants" once continued to water and feed a gift chrysanthemum after cutting off the old stems. Kept in a sunny window, it flowered in the late winter. In the spring, it was placed in a window box, where it bloomed again in the fall.

With good culture, plants will produce large blooms, even under average home conditions. After flowering, cut stems back and set pots aside in a storage room or basement window, preferably cool, and water occasionally in order to keep the roots alive. In early spring, separate the roots, and set out the new young shoots in the garden where they will flower in the fall. If the plants are not hardy, lift clumps after flowering to store in a coldframe, basement, or greenhouse for the winter. Or cover with a thick layer of straw or marsh hay if climate is not too severe. In spring divide again, plant the new divisions in the garden, and repeat the cycle each year.

Another method is to raise new plants from cuttings for pot or garden culture. Florists usually do this in the very early spring, when more bench space is available, using new, vigorous shoots that have sprouted from the base. Indoor gardeners can take cuttings earlier, selecting the strongest shoots as soon as they are large enough to handle. If plants are kept in a warm place after old stems are cut back to the roots, new growth will come along fast.

Cuttings of chrysanthemums root quickly and easily. Under good conditions, roots appear on softwood cutting in a week to ten days. Tips root best. Cut stems with a sharp knife, taking pieces about four inches long, and dip ends in a hormone powder, such as Rootone, to hasten rooting. Insert in moist sand, vermiculite, or shredded sphagnum moss—all good mediums, though sand dries out quickly.

Space cuttings two to three inches apart in trays, bulb pans, or other containers, and cover with a piece of polyethylene plastic to hold in humidity. During the rooting period, place in well-lighted windows, but not in direct sunlight. North exposure is excellent. A temperature range of 60°–65° F. is best, but cuttings will root well in the 70°–75° F. readings of the average home.

When strong root systems have developed, transplant each cutting to a two- or three-inch pot, using ordinary soil mixture. Place in a sunny window, and feed every ten days to two weeks with liquid fertilizer. Growth will be better if pots are placed on a layer of moist sand or pebbles in large trays or pans, where they will get increased amounts of humidity.

Once plants start to grow actively, keep turning containers periodically so stems will grow straight. Pinch tips to encourage side branching. In late April or early May, depending on the date of the last killing frost, set plants in the garden, giving them light, well-drained soil in a sunny location. Continue to pinch tips (or cut off several inches) until mid-July. Stake and spray as needed, and in early fall pot up clumps, which transplant easily for indoor bloom. Plants can also be grown in pots or other containers all summer, without transferring to the garden.

Chrysanthemums are so-called short-day, long-night plants. Like poinsettia and Christmas cactus, they require long periods of darkness in order to set buds and then bloom. In commercial greenhouses, they are covered with black cloth from late afternoon to early morning. Pot plants grown indoors can be forced into earlier bloom if covered with baskets or boxes at dusk.

Plants that are wintered in a cool basement or coldframe can be brought to warmth and light in late winter. When new growth appears, take cuttings or individual stems with roots to repeat the procedure for new flowering plants to enjoy in the garden or indoors.

Clerodendron

Clerodendron

(Clerodendron)

Also called glory-bower, this showy, shrubby climber, with clusters of white bracts and red flowers, is a fast grower that attains several feet in a year. A native of tropical West Africa, it can be trained as a vine or pruned hard into bush form. The most commonly grown clerodendron, *C. thompsoniae*, has oval, brown-veined leaves, dark green above, light beneath, one-and-a-half inches long. Stems are purple.

Flowers appear almost all year, but most abundantly in summer and fall. White bracts, which turn pinkish with age, appear a few weeks before the cherry-red blossoms. Rest plants after flowering by giving less water gradually—only enough to keep soil barely moist. Also prune top growth severely. Plants may lose many leaves, but will fill in with new spring growth.

Clerodendron will grow in an all-purpose soil mixture. Give plants warmth and sun, and feed in spring and summer. Provide a trellis or other support on which to climb. Cuttings taken from hardened stems (soft-wood cuttings will rot) with root in peatmoss and sand. Mealy bugs can be controlled with malathion.

The colorful hybrid *C. speciosum*, a cross between *C. splendens* and *C. thompsoniae*, has dark red bracts and bright red flowers. The shrubby *C. fragrans pleniflorum*, common in gardens in the South and suited to cool winter temperatures, has large hairy leaves and compact heads of fragrant, peach-colored flower clusters. It is native to China and Japan.

Jade Plant

(*Crassula argentea*)

If you like the bonsai effect of a small, gnarled tree, add jade plant to your collection. Familiar is the disproportionately thick, woody trunk and the heavy branches, brown in color. As plants age, they resemble miniature trees, especially if all shoots are removed from the base and only a single, main trunk remains. Japanese rubber plant, Chinese rubber plant, and Japanese laurel are other names for this tough succulent from South Africa, which may be listed as *C. argentea* or *C. arborescens*. A slow grower, it takes many years for plants to reach two or three feet.

Jade plant often comes into homes by way of florist's dish gardens. It is easily recognized by its thick, fleshy, oval, dark green leaves, shiny above. In all-day sun, as in California where it is commonly grown in gardens and in tubs on terraces, leaf edges turn rosy-red. Mature plants will occasionally, under favorable indoor conditions, produce clusters of small, fragrant, showy creamy-white flowers.

Give jade plant a sandy, well-drained soil, with little humus. Be careful not to overwater, though during the growing period keep it constantly moist. Too much water or too little will cause leaves to yellow and drop. In late fall, rest the plant by keeping soil rather dry, with only enough moisture to prevent leaves from shriveling. This will help to induce flowering on mature plants.

Repot small plants annually in early spring, but keep large specimens in the same container for three or four years. In spring, scrape soil from the surface, replace with new and follow with a normal feeding program during spring and summer. In insufficient light,

Jade plant

growth becomes lanky and leaves small; tips tend to bend over and curve upward.

Older plants require annual pruning in early spring to restrict size and induce branching. Also prune to develop a bonsai character. Tip cuttings can be rooted in peatmoss and sand or water. Syringe foliage often to keep glossy and remove dust, and spray with nicotine sulfate for mealy bugs. The variegated form *C. a. variegata*, with mottled creamy-white leaves, is somewhat tricky.

Japanese Pittosporum

(Pittosporum tobira)

Also called Australian laurel, this handsome evergreen shrub, native to China and Japan, was until recently primarily known as a garden plant in the South and on the West Coast in America, where it is often treated as a hedge. Lustrous, leathery, oval, dark green leaves, three to four inches long, form the background for terminal clusters of small creamy-white flowers, sweetly scented like orange blossoms.

Japanese pittosporum has now become a much-loved pot plant that does well under ordinary house conditions, though it prefers a cool atmosphere. Adapted to sun, shade, and even poor light, it needs sunshine in order to blossom and maintain a compact appearance. Not bothered by drafts or wintery blasts, it makes a good decorative plant for an entranceway, as often seen in large office buildings.

Japanese pittosporum grows in an average potting mixture. Keep soil barely moist, allowing it to dry out slightly between thorough soakings. Feed the plant when it is making new growth, but do not overdo it, or it will stimulate soft growth. Since it tends to become leggy, prune regularly, starting when plants are small. Take the plants outdoors to part shade in summer to build up strength for the winter. A form *P. t. variegata*, with leaves marked with white, is often grown in terrariums. Propagate both kinds by cutting.

Japanese pittosporum

Jasmine

(Jasminum)

When we speak of jasmine, we usually mean the poet's jasmine (*Jasminum officinale grandiflorum*), a shrubby vine, with fern-like leaves and small white flowers, deliciously fragrant. Native to Persia, it has long been famous in poetry and song. It is commonly planted in the Mediterranean countries; in Greece, small children sell bunches at sidewalk cafes, with each blossom impaled on a pine tree needle. Several other jasmine, or jessamines are available, all with white, starry, fragrant flowers. Some of these are true jasmines, botanically speaking, and others are not.

One true jasmine, which makes an excellent pot plant, flowering in winter and summer, is the angel wing jasmine (*J. gracile grandiflorum*). A scrambling vine, it can be pruned as a small shrub that will support itself. Its shiny, privetlike leaves form the background for starry white flowers, each with nine petals. Their scent is pleasant, not overpowering. Though each blossom remains fresh only one day, wilting the following morning and dropping by early afternoon, others keep unfolding, so plants are almost always in bloom.

The charming vine, with small white flowers that resemble pinwheels, that is called star or Confederate jasmine (*Trachelospermum jasminoides*) is not a true member of the clan. It is common in gardens in the South (hence the name Confederate jasmine) and on the West Coast. A rapid climber, growing slowly as a pot plant, it has oval, pointed, glossy, dark green leaves. It belongs to the dogbane family, but possesses a true "jasmine" fragrance.

Another is the Madagascar jasmine (*Stephanotis floribunda*), a twining vine of the milkweed family, with thick, oval, shiny green leaves, three inches long and one and a half inches wide. The tubular, creamy-white flowers, one to two inches long, are very fragrant, and are much sought for bride's bouquets for their exquisite beauty and long-lasting quality. These plants should be rested in the early winter and grown at 55° to 60° F. They perform well at warmer temperatures, but do not like high humidity. Plants need support, as they are tall, vigorous growers. Cuttings from half-ripened wood will root in sand and peat in the spring. All these jasmines need sun and an ordinary soil mixture, with extra sand or vermiculite added for good drainage. Trim excess growth in fall, when plants are brought indoors, and keep the plants cool if possible. Rest them by watering only enough to keep soil moist; give

Angel wing jasmine

them more water and start to feed as days lengthen in late January. Both the poet's and star jasmines will need support.

All make choice pot plants for the terrace in summer, where their small, sweetly scented white flowers can be enjoyed at close range, particularly in the evening.

Norfolk-Island-Pine

(Araucaria excelsa)

This is an enchanting "Christmas tree" from the tropics. For years I have been growing one successfully in a west window. On the whole, it is not considered an easy house plant, because it grows best in cool temperatures in winter and requires even moisture at its roots. Over- or underwatering can cause needles of the lower branches to shed.

A pyramidal evergreen that is native to the Pacific, Norfolk-island-Pine will usually send out a new leader each year, topped with four or five radiating branches arranged in tiered fashion. Light green needles are soft to the touch. As plants become older, branches begin to droop slightly, adding grace to the overall appearance.

If possible, grow this evergreen at 45° to 60° F in winter, as in a cool entranceway or bedroom. However, if you have no such spot for it, place in a bright window, and water with care. Give an average potting mixture, and feed in spring and summer when the plant is making new growth. Stake plants as they become taller, and shift to a larger container as needed—eventually to a tub.

At Christmas decorate your Norfolk-island-Pine with baubles, tinsel, and other decorations to turn it into a living "Christmas tree" that will be the center of attraction. Live plants are actually reminiscent of the spruces and firs of northern forests.

Another araucaria that may be purchased as a young plant is (*A. araucana*), the monkey puzzle tree, so-called because although monkeys can climb up, the stiff, prickly, oval leaves prevent them from getting down. Native to Chile, these trees attain full size in gardens in Ireland, which are warmed by the Gulf Stream.

Passion Vine

(*Passiflora*)

The early Spaniards who came to the New World were fascinated by the odd blossoms of this vine, which seemed to depict the story of the crucifixion, with ten petals representing the ten apostles; Judas, the betrayer, and Doubting Thomas are left out. The radiating filaments in the center resemble the crown-of-thorns, and the stamens are the five wounds. The three styles in the center look like nails, while the coiling tendrils are the whips by which Christ was beaten. The parted leaves, with their lobes, are shaped like the hands of the accusers. And so the exotic blossoms relate the passion, or suffering, of Christ.

The most commonly grown passion vine is *Passiflora alato-caerulea*, a handsome hybrid, with fragrant, four-inch flowers that are purple, blue, pink, and white. It will flower in a sunny window off and on all year round. Give the plant an average potting mixture, and keep the soil constantly moist. Passion vine prefers cool temperatures; in fact, it tolerates below-freezing temperatures, and in sheltered spots in southern New England plants survive winters if roots are mulched.

Given a large container, passion vine will grow handsomely and

Passion vine *(Passiflora caerulea)*

cover a wall in a short time. Stems can be trained around windows so leaves will get maximum light. Six-inch cuttings, taken in fall, can be rooted in water or sand for small plants for winter. In spring, take cuttings and root them to set out in the garden, treating them as annuals in the North.

Several other kinds of passion vines are available for the collector. Yellow granadilla or water-lemon (*P. laurifolia*) has white, red, and violet flowers, followed by large yellow fruits that are edible; this is also true of other passifloras. Maypop (*P. incarnata*), white, purple, and pink, grows from Virginia south to Florida. Most startling of all is the red and orange flowering *P. coccinea*.

The flowers of the passion vine open during the day, but close tightly at night. They are a lovely sight when floated in a shallow bowl of water. To keep the blossoms open, drop melted wax from a lighted candle at the base of the sepals and the petals. This is how florists treat the blossoms before using them in corsages and wedding bouquets.

Rubber Plant

(Ficus)

This old-time house plant, a familiar sight in parlors at the turn of the century, is now back in style. Used in homes and in plush offices, the problem with the common rubber plant (*Ficus elastica*) is that it grows too large and soon reaches the ceiling. It requires regular pruning (severed stems give off a milky sap), but after a few years of cutting back, it loses its grace. Eventually, it outgrows its container, no matter how large.

The common rubber plant, which tolerates considerable coolness, has large, elongated, shiny, leathery, dark green leaves, about a foot long. Variations include the showy *F. e. decora*, with larger leaves. The variegated types are especially attractive, as *F. e. doescheri*, gray-green and creamy-white, and *F. e. variegata*, edged with white.

Larger-leaved, but different in shape, is the less common fiddle-leaf rubber plant (*F. pandurata*), with leaves as much as 18 inches long, shaped like a violin. I have admired enormous specimens in lobbies and offices in New York City—trees said to be valued at more than $1,000 each. I am more attracted to the smaller-leaved ficus, also popular in offices, as *F. benjamina*, a tree with a broad crown and drooping habit, and *F. nitida*, more upright and compact. Both have small eliptical leaves, two to five inches long.

All ficus grow well in ordinary potting mixture. Tolerant of poor light, they perform better if given sun. The large, glossy leaves require dusting from time to time. Leggy plants can be air layered (see Chapter on propagation).

Entirely different in form and habit is the creeping fig (*F. pumila*), a vining plant with small, oval, inch-long leaves, often found clinging to greenhouse walls by means of its aerial rootlets. In India, its native habitat, it adheres to the barks of trees, as do philodendrons. A smaller-leaved form, *F. p. minima*, can be grown upright on a piece of bark or allowed to cascade in a hanging basket.

Swedish Ivy

(Plectranthus australis)

How and where the name Swedish ivy originated, I cannot say, but this easy-to-grow trailer, now common in many homes, is not an ivy, but a member of the mint family. It resembles a small green-leaved coleus, with the typical square stem.

I was introduced to Swedish ivy hardly more than five years ago. Books on house plants published within a decade do not list it. Yet today plants grace windows of restaurants and small shops, even replacing philodendron. This is understandable because Swedish ivy grows easily in any kind of light, though growth is stockier if plants receive some sun. Cuttings root quickly at any time of year; little wonder it has managed to get around.

Swedish ivy has rounded, shiny, waxy, dark green leaves, scalloped along the edges. It is a fast growing trailer that is particularly at home in a hanging basket. It tolerates heat and dry air, but needs constant pinching to keep in check. Large plants can be pruned heavily twice a year. Root cuttings in early spring or fall for new plants. Use them freely in window boxes or plant in borders to fill in bare spots, since it makes a fine annual ground cover in shade.

Prostrate coleus (*P. oertendahli*) is another species that is an equally foolproof trailer, with dark green leaves, silvery veined and tinted purple along the edges. The lavender flowers are not showy. Plants grow with equal ease, and cuttings rooted in water can be grown outdoors in summer.

Wax Plant

(Hoya carnosa)

I remember vividly a thrifty wax plant, which I admired for many years in a northwest window of a city apartment. Trained around the window frame, it grew well because of the cool air that crept through the crevices during winter. A long-time favorite, wax plant is a vine from Australia that clings with aerial rootlets on a piece of natural bark, though plants can be trained on a trellis, stake, or even pruned into a bushy form.

Wax plant

Wax plant has thick, leathery, oval, dark green leaves, three to four inches long, richly glossy. In summer, older plants display clusters of small, waxy, white flowers, with pink centers. Sweetly scented and long lasting they develop on "spurs": do not cut these after the blossoms have faded, since the new crop will appear on them the following summer.

Success with wax plant depends on winter rest. Water sparingly, just enough to prevent leaves from shriveling, and keep the plant cool. In early spring, give it more warmth, around 70° F., to stimulate new growth and flowering. Use a humusy soil, as you would for begonias. However, plants will grow in an ordinary mixture.

The form *H. c. variegata* has light green leaves edged with white. On new leaves these areas are pink; they turn white later. Plants grown in sun retain the pinkish cast for a longer time. A slow grower, this form has fragrant, creamy-white flowers, with dark centers, that appear sparingly.

Delightful is the miniature wax plant (*H. bella*) from India, with similar oval, pointed leaves, only an inch long. More dwarf in habit, the aromatic waxy white flowers appear generously during the summer months. All kinds can be grown in a hanging basket. Hoyas respond to generous watering and feeding during the summer growing period. Spray with malathion when plants are plagued with scale or mealy bugs.

(4)

Sunless North Windows

Growing plants in shady north windows is a challenge. Yet when it comes to choices, nature has been more generous than we realize, with a wide selection of tropical foliage plants that thrive in the deep shade of large forest trees in their native habitats.

If these plants are exposed to full sun, their leaves become coarse, forfeiting their delicacy. This is true with coleus. The foliage of others, such as wax begonias, turns reddish, while some plants become yellowish, among them philodendrons. In gardens, hardy ferns, pachysandras, hostas, and sweet woodruff are shade lovers whose leaves turn an unsightly, sickly, yellow if they are grown in full sun. Yet culturally speaking, these plants are healthy.

North light is even light. Its intensity is uniform, except when the sun disappears behind clouds. At north windows, you do not have to draw shades or move plants back to avoid "scorching," as with plants in sunny exposures. The closer plants are placed to window panes, however, the stronger the light. In north exposure, a light meter will record less variation than in sunny windows, where plants close to windows are in full sun, while others a few feet away are in complete shade.

Though I have indicated that north windows are "sunless," this is not entirely accurate. In midsummer, due north exposures receive a little sunshine in the early morning shortly after the sun rises and in the late afternoon, just before the sun sets. Yet this amount of sunshine, though it contributes to healthy plant growth, is negligible.

In order for north windows to receive the full percentage of this sunshine, they must not be shaded by nearby buildings or trees. Since sunshine enters north windows at a sharp angle, and then moves quickly away, only those plants on window sills or stands near windows benefit from the direct rays of the sun. This does not imply that other plants, located farther back, do not profit from the increased amounts of light in summer.

The sharp difference between south and north exposures may be likened to black and white, but is not as drastic as it may sound when it comes to the growing of plants. This is because north light, if completely open and not obstructed by trees or buildings, is strong light. Climbing roses will grow magnificently on the north side of the house, and I have often seen luxurious north-facing window boxes with sun-loving geraniums, marigolds, and petunias. In summer, house plants will grow better at "open" north windows than at east, south, or west exposures that are shaded by large trees.

North windows are often better suited to the year-round growing of plants than are east, south, and west because the plants do not dry out as quickly. The person who works and likes to travel should keep this in mind. At north windows, there is no reflected heat, while temperatures at south windows will jump several degrees when the sun is shining, winter or summer.

Northeast and southwest exposures belong in the "north" category. Whatever sunshine they receive from spring to fall is of short duration and "cool" in intensity. Actually, windows that are shaded by nearby buildings have similar amounts of light, whether they face north, east, south, or west.

Plants at north windows benefit from light that reflects from adjacent buildings, particularly if they are white or light colored. An African violet enthusiast, who grows prizewinning plants at north windows, attributes her success largely to the light that bounces off her neighbor's house in both winter and summer.

North light is intriguing. Among the four exposures it is the most challenging from the point of view of successful plant growth. I think of east and west as fraternal twins, and south and north as siblings, similar yet opposite. North light does not glow yet imparts its own subtle allure, unique and mystifying. The following plants grow well in a northern exposure:

Caladium

Caladium

(*Caladium*)

It would be difficult to name a plant with more colorful leaves than the fancy-leaved caladium. Some varieties are so brilliantly hued, they defy description. They have large, heart-shaped leaves that vary from red, rose, and pink to white, and all are veined with green.

Caladiums, which are members of the arum family, are warmth-loving bulbous plants, usually grown for summer color, both indoors or out. They need heat and humidity. Give tubers an early start—in March or April. Place the tubers in bulb pans or flats in a mixture of peat and sand, covering the tops with two inches of the medium. Keep moist, but not wet, as overwatering induces rotting. Bulbs need warmth to start, 75° to 85° F.; if the temperature drops below 70° F. they stand still.

When roots have developed and tops are six inches high, shift bulbs to individual five- or six-inch pots, or put them directly in the containers where they are to grow. Use a rich, humusy soil: one part loam, one part peatmoss or leaf mold, one-half part dry manure or a heavy sprinkling of mixed fertilizer. With hot weather, plants grow quickly. Give strong light (or weak sunshine) for intense leaf coloring.

Culture during the growing period is simple. Keep soil constantly moist, as roots resent drying out, and feed every two weeks with liquid fertilizer. Turn pots around regularly; otherwise leaves will face the source of light; turning should be done daily with indoor plants if the light is very weak. Insufficient light will result in smaller leaves, with broader outer margins and paler coloring.

By late summer, older leaves start to turn black at the base of the stems and droop over, before turning yellow. When most leaves have shriveled, decrease watering, finally withholding it entirely. After all leaves have turned brown, remove tubers and place them in dry peat-moss, sand, or vermiculite. Or they can be left in their pots. Store bulbs at 60° to 65° F. or slightly higher; start into growth again the following spring. Varieties of caladiums are numerous, like the exotic John Peed, metallic red and green; Mrs. M. F. Joyner, rose and white; Roehr's Dawn, white with rose veins; Candidum, green and white, one of the most familiar; Pink Bonnet, a dwarf type with pink leaves edged with green. *Caladium humboldti* is a miniature, with green leaves heavily spotted with white. This one keeps on growing and is not inclined to go dormant.

Coleus

(Coleus)

Like fancy-leaved caladium, coleus provides dazzling colors with their leaves, which are smaller than caladium leaves but equally evocative. In summer it can be grown in the garden in shade, which should not be too dense. Without sufficient light, outdoors or in, growth becomes leggy and leaves grow smaller and less brilliant. In very deep shade, the lower leaves also tend to drop prematurely.

Coleus, a member of the mint family, is an easy-to-grow, short-lived tropical plant. A native of the East Indies, it sports multihued leaves in red and pink, yellow and gold, green and white—with many variations. It prefers a humusy soil and a warm, humid atmosphere, but it will thrive even where the air is dry.

To prevent legginess, pinch frequently, and cut back hard before new spring growth. Coleus requires more water than most house plants, and wilts when allowed to go dry; lower leaves drop if this

Coleus

happens too often. It roots easily in water or moist sand, or it can be grown from seed, an adventurous experience because a single packet results in a wide variety of colors and leaf forms.

Sow seed in vermiculite or other medium, and keep it evenly moist, avoiding overwatering as wetness causes rotting. Keep at 65° F., and give young seedlings strong light to prevent spindly growth. Transplant after a few sets of leaves develop. If seedlings tend to flower, remove the flower spikes, as this induces bushier growth.

New coleus varieties in separate colors listed in seed catalogs vie with petunias, marigolds, and zinnias among what is new. Some of the more distinctive are the yellow-green Chartreuse; Firebird, orange-red edged with green: Othello, called the Black Coleus; and such strains as Oriental Splendor and Rainbow, with separate classifications known as Golden; Pink; Candidum, cream and ivory; and Velvet, a bright, glowing red.

English Ivy

(Hedera helix)

English ivy, widely grown as a vine and ground cover in European gardens, is an evergreen climber, with lobed, glossy leaves. It is long-lived and hardy even in the North, and specimen plants with thick trunks may be centuries old. It is the ivy made famous in English literature—the "yonder ivy-mantled tower" of Gray's haunting "Elegy Written in a Country Churchyard." In gardens it clings to barks of trees and brick walls by means of aerial rootlets.

Though a common house plant, English ivy is not the easiest house plant to grow to perfection, because it prefers a cool atmosphere. Leaves are also plagued by red spider, particularly if the air is dry and temperatures are over 70° F.

If cool temperatures cannot be provided, give all ivies that stem from the genus *Hedera* a frequent shower. Do not overwater. Allow soil to dry out a bit between waterings. Plants thrive best in bright light, not necessarily direct sunshine, and may be kept in hallways or entrance-ways, as they do not mind chilly drafts in winter.

Ivies thrive in average potting mixture or in a 50-50 combination of light, sandy soil and peatmoss. Strands may also be grown in water for decoration on mantels, shelves, wall brackets, or even hanging baskets. Variations are numerous, with leaves that differ in size and form and colors ranging from solid greens to combinations of light green, gray, yellow and gold, cream and white. For the collector the list is extensive.

Appealing is Baby Ivy (*H. h. minor*), with dainty leaves veined with gray. Silvery veined is the fast-growing, small-leaved *H. h. pedata*.

H. h. cordata, with heart-shaped leaves, is a slow grower. Other variations with expressive names include Gold Dust, mottled yellow and green leaves; Feather, deeply cut small leaves; Curly Locks, curled and crested dark green leaves; Sweetheart, heart-shaped leaves; Garland, pleated dark green leaves; Fleur, wavy leaves, and Glacier, gray-green leaves edged with white.

If you have Irish blood or are simply addicted to the Emerald Isle, consider the vigorous, large-leaved variety, *H. h. hibernica*; Shamrock, a small-leaved, compact form; and Irish Lace, tiny, delicate, dainty, with deeply lobed leaves.

In addition to the English, another ivy to grow is the variegated Canary Islands ivy (*Hedera canariensis variegata*), with larger, rounded, leathery leaves, blotched creamy-white. In one way it is easier, because

76

it tolerates higher temperatures. Its nearly white leaves add sparkle to groupings of solid-green foliage plants. Also called Algerian ivy, it needs strong light.

Another variation is *H. c. aureo-maculata* with larger leaves speckled with golden-yellow. These two forms frequently come in florist dish gardens. If taken out and potted individually, they make distinctive pot plants, with a flair of their own.

Ferns

If I were a collector, among house plants ferns would be my choice. Ferns comprise a graceful group of foliage plants that thrive on little light and require humidity for best growth. In recent years they have staged a remarkable comeback in popularity, among them the Boston fern, which is now used constantly by a large Boston hotel to decorate its lobby. For soft greenery, delicacy of pattern, rhythm and grace, and a feeling of refreshing "coolness," ferns are in a class by themselves.

Ferns require a rich, humusy soil—one-third sandy loam, one-third peatmoss or leaf mold, and one-third coarse sand. Give them good light, but little or no sun. A north window is ideal, but in midwinter when the sun is weak, they can be placed in sunny exposures, particularly if they are shielded by thin curtains or Venetian blinds.

Ferns need moisture. Slightly wet soil is better than dry, yet good drainage is important. Water should flow out freely so it is wise to use plenty of chards at repotting time. Apply more water during periods of active growth. For top performance, ferns also need humidity, around 70%, though some, like the staghorn and the holly ferns, thrive in dry air. To increase humidity, rest the pots on trays with moist pebbles, and sprinkle foliage often. Use mechanical humidifiers if possible. Placing a layer of moist sphagnum moss on the surface of the soil of plants is helpful.

In spring and summer feed ferns every two weeks with liquid fertilizer, preferably half strength. Select a high-nitrogen formula to promote lush foliage growth. If your ferns are taken outdoors in summer, place them in complete shade. Indoors, ferns grow well at 60° to 75° F.

The kinds to grow is much a matter of taste. The Boston fern (*Nephrolepis exaltata bostoniensis*) is dependable, and so is its smaller, upright form, Trevillian. Less demanding is the bird's next fern (*Asplenium nidus*). Hardly resembling a fern at all, it has long, waxy fronds that are apt to turn brown along the edges if air is too dry. It is a rapid grower that is never static or dull.

Holly fern (*Cyrtomium falcatum*) also does not look like a fern. It has

77

Boston ferns

leathery, dark green fronds, jagged along the edges like the leaves of holly. Tough and long lasting, it is one of the easiest to grow as a house plant. Squirrel's foot fern (*Davallia bullata*) has feathery, glossy fronds and neat, gray, furry rhizomes, like the feet of a squirrel. Larger growing is the hare's foot fern (*Polypodium aureum*), with deeply cut, blue-green, arching fronds and creeping rhizomes. Both are often grown in hanging baskets.

The list of ferns is extensive, so select according to preferences. To control mealy bugs and scale, two common pests particularly difficult to eradicate on ferns, use wettable malathion, since the emulsifiable forms injure the leaves. And avoid all oil sprays.

Gold-Dust Plant

(Aucuba japonica variegata)

The variegated form of the gold-dust plant, with large, dark green leaves, heavily spotted with gold, is the aucuba most commonly grown as a house plant. A very handsome shrub, it will attain two or three feet if given a large container. The oval leaves, six to seven inches long, are glossy and roughly toothed at the ends, with spots of varying size and color intensity.

Japanese laurel is another name for this easy-to-grow broad-leaved evergreen. It makes a superb specimen plant in an unheated breezeway or room, since it tolerates below-freezing temperatures. As a house plant, keep it in a cool window; however, it grows remarkably well at 70° F. or higher.

This aucuba is often planted in Japanese dish gardens. Like jade and snake plants, if removed and repotted it will develop into a long-lived and undemanding house plant. Give it an average potting mixture, and water it to keep soil evenly moist. Allow soil to dry out a bit between waterings in winter, when growth is less active. Its red fruits last a long time if plants are kept cool. Cuttings from half-ripened wood root in peatmoss and sand. Sprinkle the foliage periodically, and pinch the tips to keep the plant compact.

Many variations of the Japanese shrub are available, among them *A. j. goldiana*, with yellow centers in the leaves; *A. j. dentata*, with coarsely toothed leaves; the broad-leaved *A. j. macrophylla*; and a newcomer from Japan, *A. j. Fuiri Aoki*, with yellow leaves accented with green in the centers.

Grape and Kangaroo Ivies

(Cissus)

These two rugged plants, though not true ivies, are climbers that may be given trellises or allowed to hang over gracefully on a table, wall bracket, planter, or hanging basket.

Grape ivy (*Cissus rhombifolia*) is the more common. Unmindful of heat, dry air, and subdued light, it does object to frequent drying out,

Grape ivy

which causes its foliage to wilt, dry up, and fall. The leaves, made up of three leaflets, are pointed, toothed and glossy above, and hairy and rust-colored beneath.

Also not mindful of heat and arid atmosphere, the kangaroo ivy (*C. antarctica*) from Australia is somewhat more difficult. As a vine, it climbs by means of tendrils, and has oval, slightly toothed leaves, shiny above and three to four inches long. A miniature form is available.

A less-known cissus for the collector is cape grape (*C. capensis*), a tuberous species, much planted in southern California. Young kidney-shaped leaves are covered with pinkish hairs, which disappear with age. Leaves are rusty beneath.

Also unusual is the tuberous *C. adenopodus*, a rapid grower from tropical Africa. Its three-parted leaves, up to six inches long, are hairy and green above, red below. It prefers warmth and humidity. *C. striata* is a novelty, a tendril vine from South America, with leaves of three to five leaflets. It is similar to grape ivy, but smaller.

Most striking of all is *C. discolor*, from Java, common in old-time greenhouses. The heart-shaped, six-inch long leaves taper to a graceful point. Finely toothed, they are velvety green above, mottled with silvery white and tinged with pink. Underneath they are reddish-purple colored.

Give cissus a general or a high-humus mixture as befits its jungle heritage. Most like to be kept moist, although tuberous kinds need to be rested after growth has ceased; keep the soil on the dry side for a few months, usually in the fall and early winter. Pinch back regularly, and do not hesitate to cut long shoots to the base when they lose their lower leaves.

Lily of the Nile

(Agapanthus africanus)

From the Cape of Good Hope comes this old-fashioned tub plant, cherished for its clusters of funnel flowers that are true blue in color. Large estates in past decades invariably grew large specimens of this member of the lily family, also called African lily, along with oleander, sweet bay (*Laurus nobilis*), Chinese hibiscus, camellia, and blue hydrangea.

Tuberous-rooted agapanthus has leathery, shiny, strap-like, arching leaves up to three feet long. Since they are evergreen, plants are attractive even when not in bloom. Long flower stems may support as many as thirty two-inch blossoms, which usually appear in summer, a lovely, refreshing sight in warm weather.

This imposing plant requires ample space indoors in winter. Place it in a corner by a bright picture window or in a spare room that is cool. Begin to decrease watering after flowering, and in winter keep soil on the dry side in order to let the plant rest.

Agapanthus can remain in the same container for several years, if it is given liquid fertilizer when flower stems appear. Divide large plants before new growth starts, and place the tops of the fleshy root-stocks even with the soil line in an average potting mixture.

Available is a white form *A. a. albidus*, and the dwarf, compact *A. a. nanus*, frequently seen in California gardens, often in pots. On the West Coast, agapanthus is a durable ground cover, commonly planted in narrow strips along highways, where it tolerates fumes from the exhaust pipes of automobiles.

Peperomia

(*Peperomia*)

There are many wonderful kinds of these small, low-growing foliage plants, members of the pepper family. The name, which comes from the Greek, refers to their kinship to the true pepper. As a group, they do best in bright light, preferring shading from strong sun, which discolors the fleshy leaves. Give general potting mixture and constant moisture, with good drainage, as too much wetness causes rotting at the base.

Peperomias also like warmth, which makes them good candidates for the average home. They like humidity but will probably grow well if their other needs are not overlooked. Feed these plants to aid new growth, and repot as needed. Propagate by stem or leaf cuttings.

Most familiar of all, often planted in florist's dish gardens, is pepper face (*Peperomia obtusifolia*), a trailing plant, which roots at the nodes when grown outdoors in warm regions. Native to tropical America, it has rounded, thick, glossy, waxy, dark green leaves, two to three inches broad, on fleshy stems that stay upright on small plants. As stems become longer, they need support. Two forms offer bright touches of "color," *P. o. variegata*, with light green leaves spattered with creamy-white, and *P. o. alba*, with leaves that are almost entirely white.

Also popular is the showier watermelon begonia (*P. sandersi*), from Brazil, which is not a begonia at all. Unlike pepper face, it is not a trailer, but has fleshy, heart-shaped leaves marked with silver bands on a light green background; the leaves emanate from a single crown. Leaf stems are red. A form, *P. s. argyreia*, is lighter colored between the veins. This, too, is found in florist's dish gardens.

Less likely to appear is *P. maculosa*, from Santo Domingo, with large, ovate, waxy, blue-green leaves, veined with green and white and spotted with purple-brown. Leaf stems have purple spots. From Ecuador comes *P. velutina*, an erect species with thick, ovate, dark green leaves, white veined above and reddish beneath: stems are red. From Peru hails *P. scandens*, a fast-growing creeper, with waxy, heart-shaped, light green leaves on brownish stems. Its form *P. s. variegata* sports smaller green and creamy-white leaves. Especially intriguing is *P. hederifolia*, with ruffled, rounded, glossy, metallic, gray-green leaves and contrasting red stems.

Pick-a-Back-Plant

(Tolmiaea menziesi)

Though hardly rare, this is a novelty plant that even appeals to children because of the plantlets that appear at the ends of the leaf stems at the base of the mature leaves. Its other common names are piggy-back-plant and mother-of-thousands.

Pick-a-back-plant is a low-growing ground cover, native to the West Coast, from Alaska to California. It therefore withstands cold temperatures, yet is amazingly adaptable when grown indoors. Give it a rich soil, well supplied with organic matter, and a bright window. Strong sun gives leaves a yellowish cast and turns edges brown.

Pick-a-back has leaves more or less heart-shaped two to three inches long, jagged along the edges. They are hairy and pale green in coloring, refreshing when plants are well grown. Small green flowers may appear in nodding bunches, but I have never seen them. These plants can be grown in a hanging basket or in water. They look particularly well in a compote, with runners hanging over the sides.

For best results keep them constantly moist; leaf edges turn brown if plants dry out too often. And when allowed to dry out completely, the entire plant collapses. It will revive shortly after it has been watered. Red spider mite can be controlled with kelthane. If plants that are grown in shade have yellowish leaves, feed them with a high-nitrogen fertilizer or one with such trace elements as magnesium, boron, and iron. The plantlets will root in water or sand and peatmoss, making new plants to replace those that are old and tired-looking.

Prayer Plant

(*Maranta leuconeura kerchoveana*)

Here is a fascinating low-growing plant, with spotted, oval leaves that fold upward at night, like hands in prayer, a feature that appeals to adults and children. Young plants are often sold in supermarkets, along with the larger *M. leuconeura*, heavily marked with chocolate brown spots on the new leaves, which later turn dark green.

Taller is the rarer tuberous *M. bicolor*, with six-inch oval leaves, accented with a light central strip and brown spots; it is purple on the undersides. Small white flowers, as with the common prayer plant, are not conspicuous.

Prayer plant, peacock plant, and siderasis

More striking is the related fleshy-rooted peacock plant (*Calathea makoyana*), with leaves that exhibit a fine network of veins and are decorated with dark green spots. Leaves are reddish beneath, and leaf stems are dark red.

Zebra plant (*C. zebrina*) has emerald-green leaves, with light and dark green stripes, bronzy-red on the undersides. In its native Brazil it reaches three feet, but remains six inches under cultivation. *C. ornata* hails from Ecuador, where it grows to eight feet or more in the moist jungles. As a pot plant it attains 18 inches. It has waxy, dull green leaves, reddish beneath, striped pink and white when young.

This *marantad*, a name applied to the group, requires warmth and humidity; the others are accommodating house plants. Tolerant of dry air, they like warmth; temperatures below 50° F. injure their foliage. Give them strong light for leaves to "color" well. Keep soil moist, and provide good drainage, as roots resent a stagnant condition. From December to February the soil can be kept barely moist, since the plants are resting. Though the common prayer plant will lose most of its leaves, new shoots will appear from the roots in early spring.

The dormant period is the time to divide large plants or to repot them, using a light, friable soil, like that recommended for begonias. Common pests—mealy bugs and red spider mites—which lodge on the undersides of the leaves, can be sprayed with malathion. I have observed that in early July, when days are still long, the common prayer plant will fold its leaves as early as 6 P.M. while the sun is still shining.

Spathiphyllum

(*Spathiphyllum*)

Not the least of the charms of this gracefully arching plant, with its long, shiny, dark green leaves radiating like a fountain, are the small, white calla lily-shaped blossoms perched at the tips of slender stems like doves in flight. This aroid, related to philodendron and caladium, zoomed to popularity after World War II, and is now seen in hotel lobbies, banks, offices, and homes, where it is often used in planters in combination with other tropical foliage plants.

Small-growing *Spathiphyllum patini* is recommended for homes because it takes up little space. Native to Colombia, it has narrow, sword-like leaves up to a foot long and one and a half inches wide. Tips that turn brown in winter because of dry air can be cut off with scissors.

Spathiphyllum patini

S. floribundum has shorter leaves, six inches long, but wider, two and a half inches broad, giving a dwarfer appearance. Larger is the regal *S. commutatum*, which grows over three feet tall, in time requiring a large pot or small tub.

Spathiphyllums are heat lovers, preferring temperatures in the upper sixties and higher. They can be watered less in winter, when resting, but are moisture lovers that droop if allowed to dry out. If this occurs too often, leaf tips and edges will turn brown. Syringe and dust leaves frequently. Large plants can be divided in the early spring and potted in a rich, humusy soil mixture. Divisions usually wilt and outer leaves turn yellow, but plants soon recover and start making new growth.

Spider Plant

(Chlorophytum)

Here is a tough foliage plant that can be neglected for a long period of time. It has long, slender, gracefully arching leaves, which give the effect of a spider. The name is also appropriate because the plantlets at the tips of the long stems, on which small white flowers appear, help to impart an overall spidery appearance.

When grown outdoors as a ground cover in regions where it is hardy, the long trailing stems root at the base of the plantlets. As pot plants, chlorophytums are often grown in hanging baskets. Its stems hang limply downward because of the weight of the plantlets. Plants can also be placed on shelves, tables, wall brackets, or in bird cages as a curiosity.

This member of the lily family, native to South Africa, tolerates poor light, but appreciates moisture at its fleshy, bulbous roots. It can be grown in warm or cool temperatures. Give spider plant (or ribbon plant, as it is also called) an average potting mixture. Keep the soil evenly moist, and feed when plants are growing actively. Specimens in hanging baskets should be turned around every week for symmetrical growth. Increase by dividing old crowns or by rooting plantlets at the end of the stems.

Chlorophytum comosum has foot-long green leaves, which are narrower on plants grown in dim light. Its form *C. c. mandaianum* has broad leaves, striped with white; *C. c. picturatum* has stripes of yellow along the centers of the ribbony leaves. *C. elatum*, with its foot-long green leaves is familiar, but more widely grown is its variegated form, *C. e. vittatum*, which has slender leaves striped with creamy-white through the centers. Small specimens are often included in Japanese dish gardens. Another variation, *C. e. variegatum*, has broader leaves that are mostly white. All chlorophytums make good house plants. Use them freely as trailers in planters. Scale can be controlled with malathion.

Strawberry Begonia

(Saxifraga sarmentosa)

This is an oldtime window plant, frequently grown in hanging baskets and also called strawberry geranium; it is not a strawberry, nor a begonia, nor a geranium. "Strawberry" alludes to the small runners the plants send out, and both "begonia" and "geranium" refer to the leaf similarity of these two plants. Mother-of-thousands and old man's beard are other common names.

This perennial creeper from China and Japan forms a ground cover in gardens where it is hardy. Often planted under large shade trees, it has rounded, hairy leaves two to four inches across, on long stems. Dark olive green above, they are veined with silvery white and are reddish-purple beneath. In spring and summer, plants send forth upright, long-stemmed sprays of small, long-lasting white flowers that create a misty appearance. Plantlets that develop at the tips of the runners can be cut off and rooted to form new plants to replace old specimens.

Strawberry begonia grows in an average potting mixture, but responds to a light, humusy mixture, as recommended for begonias and other fibrous-rooted plants. Keep moist, and grow as cool as possible, since it can withstand considerable cold. Shield the foliage from strong sun.

Equally appealing is the smaller form *S. s. tricolor*, with variegated leaves edged with white and pink. Also called Magic Carpet, it is less vigorous and more difficult to grow. The coloring on the undersides of the leaves is deeper. Another variety, Maroon Beauty, has larger leaves, more intense in coloring.

Twelve Apostles

(Neomarica)

This old-fashioned plant graced many a window in past years. I always grew it as a youngster, and was charmed, if not by the fan-like spread of the leaves, by the common name—twelve apostles. Many is the time

88

Twelve apostles
I counted, finding to my dismay, that my plants sometimes had more
than twelve leaves.

If you are looking for something easy, yet different, grow twelve
apostles. You might not be able to buy a plant; but keep asking your
friends and acquaintances for a slip, and in time you will find one.
Apostle plant and house and winter iris are other common names, the
last two referring to the iris-like blossoms of this member of the iris
family.

Most commonly grown is *Neomarica* (formerly *Marica*) *northiana*
from Brazil, which has flattened, glossy, light green leaves, two to
three feet tall and an inch or two wide. Mature plants send forth shoots
on which appear fragile, fragrant iris blossoms, white with blue tips
and brown at the base. The fact that each lasts but a day adds an aura
of mystery.

After the flowers fade, young plantlets appear at the tops of the flower stems, which make new plants if cut off and placed in water or sand to root. Another method of propagation is to divide large plants at repotting time, removing the smaller plants at the base. Many like to keep cutting these off large plants in order to have a single, uncluttered spreading fan of leaves. Smaller is *N. gracilis*, with one-and-a-half-foot-long leaves one inch wide, and two-inch flowers, blue, yellow, brown, or white. Native from Mexico to Brazil, it is hardy in gardens in warm regions of the country.

Neomaricas are undemanding foliage plants. Unlike others in that category which are coarse, such as snake plant and aspidistra, they have a leafy grace. Narrow plants, with their spread of sword-shaped leaves, fit comfortably on narrow window sills. They grow well without sun. Give them any ordinary soil mixture, and keep them moist, though drying out is not harmful.

Wandering Jew

(*Tradescantia fluminensis*)

Inch-plant is another name for this old-fashioned trailer, which grows luxuriantly in poor light if given a rich soil. Easy and fast-growing, it is frequently grown in water, its sprawling, spindly stems often a familiar sight on office desks and living room mantels. Oval, shiny, bright green leaves, about an inch long, are spaced an inch apart on jagged stems. Knobby nodes send forth roots quickly if cuttings are placed in water or in the garden, where it forms a ground cover for the summer in the North and grows as a permanent plant in warm climates. Inch-plant grows in any soil, but responds to the stimulus of a rich mixture. It can be grown in cool or warm temperatures, and makes a superb hanging basket plant in shade.

Among the many forms of this native of the forests of Central and South America, where it sprawls over the ground and clambers up shrubs and stumps, are the green and creamy white *T. f. variegata*; the yellow *T. f. Gold Leaf*; and the larger-leaved *T. f. albo-vittata*, with blue-green leaves, striped white, commonly called Giant White Inch Plant.

Other members of the variable clan make equally easy house plants, all belonging to the spiderwort family (*Commelinaceae*). The flowering inch-plant (*T. blossfeldiana*) is a vigorous grower, with larger, waxy

Zebrina

green leaves, hairy and purple on the undersides. Lavender-pink flowers appear in spring and summer; its variegated form is lovely. Similar is zebrina (*Zebrina pendula*), a native of Mexico, with glistening leaves, dramatically striped with purple and silver on the uppersides, but purple on the undersides. Leaf coloring is more intense in the sun. Its sports include Z. *p. discolor*, with brownish leaves, purple and silver striped: Z. *p. d. multicolor*, pinkish-cream and red; and Z. *p. minima*, small-leaved with silver stripes on a dark red background.

From Mexico, Z. *purpusi*, a vigorous grower, has fleshy leaves, olive-green and purple above, deeper purple beneath, and is recommended for a wall bracket or a hanging basket. Of recent appearance are *Setcreasea purpurea* Purple Heart, with large, deep purple leaves, and *Siderasis fuscata* (*Tradescantia fuscata*), with broad, hairy, brown leaves, accented with silvery bands along the midveins. The latter grows as a rosette, and has blue-purple flowers.

Moses-on-a-raft (*Rhoeo discolor*), an old-timer, is different because it is upright. Long, narrow, metallic-green leaves, purple on the undersides, provide background for small, white flowers in boat-like bracts, which account for the common name. Native to Mexico, it has become naturalized in the South, and is a weedy ground cover in Florida.

Other descriptive names for it are: Moses-in-the-cradle, Moses-in-the-bulrushes, three-men-in-a-boat, and purple-leaved spiderwort. The form *R. d. vittata* has thick blue-green leaves, purplish underneath, with yellow length-wise stripes on the upper sides.

You may have to search to locate a plant of the bygone *Spironema fragrans* (*Tradescantia dracaenoides*). Also upright in the form of a rosette, with broad, fleshy, sword-shaped leaves, like a gigantic tradescantia, it sends out runners with plantlets, making it an outstanding hanging basket plant. Small white flowers are intensely fragrant. This native of Mexico grows in any kind of soil and scoffs at mistreatment.

(5)

The Decorative Exposure

I am calling the fifth exposure decorative. Though at one time house plants were placed mainly at or near windows in order to benefit from sun and light, today they are used widely throughout the house simply for decoration. Many plants thrive on existing light, which is comprised of indirect daylight and the artificial illumination lamps, both fluorescent and incandescent. This is a relatively new concept. When I was growing up, we never thought of "growing" plants on the dining-room sideboard or table or on mantels, bookcases, or corner tables in the living-room. Since plants needed light—the more the better—they were congregated around windows, usually the sunniest. The plant lover who had at least one room with bay windows was considered fortunate.

Today we have a wide variety of foliage plants from dimly lit jungles of the world at our disposal for the decorative exposure, some of recent introduction, among them schefflera and *Philodendron panduraeforme*. Today we realize, too, that house plants are expendable. Particularly the permanent foliage types have come to be just another item on the household budget. Think of the geraniums, fuchsias, begonias, and lantanas we buy to plant in our gardens in the spring, and then allow to die with a hard frost. With grandmother this was unthinkable. Geraniums were lifted and suspended from the ceilings of cool dirt cellars for the winter. Other permanent plants, such as lemon verbena, wax begonia, and rosemary, were stored in cool rooms, while today we treat them as annuals.

Modern architecture has been influential in establishing the trend

93

toward decorating the house plants. Much wall space in homes, as well as offices, is devoted to glass. The picture window is a common feature, and even kitchens have glass that extends from the ceiling to the floor. In new office buildings, a greater amount of space is devoted to glass, and in New York and other cities, it is not uncommon for ten-foot-tall ficus and scheffleras to flourish in the bright daylight of lobbies and plush offices.

Another factor that helped to evolve the decorative exposure is the increased amounts of artificial lighting. Our homes and places of business are brightly lit. In offices, lights are switched on all day long, even in rooms with direct sunshine. In some cases, automatic timers go on when light intensity becomes low. In our homes, it is not unusual to light up every room of the house until the last person retires. There are also special set-ups for house plants with lights that are kept on for several hours during the day and night.

How far away from windows does decorative exposure begin? Six or ten feet? At least that, though it depends on the sizes of the windows. For the most part, the rays of the sun do not strike plants that are used decoratively, except perhaps in the early morning or the late afternoon.

The underlying principle of the decorative exposure is the use of plants freely throughout every room of the house. It is important to select the right kinds of plants. These are generally foliage types. However, chrysanthemums, Easter lilies, cyclamen, azaleas, or other flowering specimens are sometimes introduced for seasonal color.

If veriegated waxplant is attractive on a coffee table, then use it without further deliberation. If a grouping of dumb canes and pothos forms an interesting pattern on a dining room sideboard and dracaenas and scheffleras add warmth to an entrance hall, then arrange them carefully for the best effect. And philodendrons in wall brackets in the bathroom might add just the touch that is needed. Since decorative possibilities with house plants are limitless, use them freely. Place them on shelves, mantels, desks, television and stereo sets, dressers, steps, and pedestals. Rest tall specimens on the floor to fill an empty corner or soften the bareness of a wide expanse of wall. The following plants are useful for decorative purposes and will thrive in little light.

Aglaonema

(Aglaonema)

For the person who likes to grow plants in water, this is a number-one candidate. One of the stubbornest of foliage plants, the most common variety is the Chinese evergreen (*Aglaonema simplex*). Other aglaonemas, with their heart-, arrow-, or lance-shaped leaves, often blotched or marked, are far more interesting. They resemble dumb canes, for which they are often mistaken. Like them, these arums fare well on dim light, and are frequently used in planters in homes and business places. Insignificant calla-shaped flowers are made up of a white spathe and spadix.

Chinese evergreen (*A. simplex*) hardly needs any introduction. Its leathery, lance-shaped, dark green leaves are wavy along the margins. It loses its lower leaves as it develops, eventually becoming leggy; but if tops are cut off, they can be rooted in water. Allowed to develop,

Chinese evergreen

they curve and twist in fascinating fashion. Add small plants of philo-dendron and pothos at the base of these plants to cover the bare stems.

Several years ago I had a plant of *A. robelini*. When the lower leaves turned yellow and were removed, tops were cut off and placed in water, where they remained for several years, sending forth new, smaller leaves. No fertilizer was added. This vigorous aglaonema has leaves marked with light traces of silver. Also highly decorative is *A. costatum* from Malaya; it is low growing, with large, white-spotted, gray-green leaves, up to eight inches long and four inches wide.

Ceylon is the home of *A. commutatum*, characterized with leathery, six-inch-long leaves, accented with pate green and silver. Its intriguing form *A. c. albo-variegata* has white canes and leaf stems. *A. bospitum* from Thailand displays leathery, dark green leaves with creamy-white spots. More unusual is *A. oblongifolium*, which has stiff, foot-and-a-half-long, dark green leaves on extra-long petioles.

Australian Umbrella Tree

(*Schefflera actinophylla*)

It is not too many years ago that this native of Australia and Java began to adorn our homes and places of business. Among tropical foliage plants, large or small, few equal it for spectacular, elegant beauty. A member of the aralia family, its huge glossy compound leaves, spread like the outstretched fingers of the hand. In the jungle it attains thirty feet. Attached to long stems, the leaves are made up of six to eight leaflets, six to eight inches long.

Though schefflera grows in warm, humid forests, in almost pure humus, it is an adaptable plant that fortunately does not mind hot, dry air of apartments and offices. This plus its unique beauty make it one of the outstanding "finds" of the first half of the century. It will grow in any kind of soil and in subdued light. Keep the soil moist, but do not overwater, as this may cause stems to rot. Feed the plants while growth is active, and shift them to larger containers when needed, using an ordinary soil mixture. With a moist cloth remove dust from the shiny leaf surfaces periodically.

Prune the tips to stimulate branching, and make new plants by air layering. (See Chapter 7 for directions.) Yellowish, streaky foliage may be due to red spider mites, which can be killed by directing kelthane or another miticide to the under-surfaces of the leaves.

Australian umbrella tree lends a smart, sophisticated touch to contemporary interiors. Because it grows large, it will eventually require a sizable pot or tub. Plants are ideal in rooms with high ceilings or offices with good light. Commonly seen in south Florida gardens is the similar *Brassaia actinophylla*. Taller growing, it is frequently used in the landscaping of modern churches and public buildings.

Bromeliads

(*Bromeliacaea*)

Bromeliads are marvellous plants that have everything in their favor. Characterized by oddly shaped leaves, with strange and bizarre markings, they are very easy to grow, and are practically immune to all kinds of neglect. Since they are very slow growing they are expensive, and so remain little known. One bromeliad, however, that actually costs nothing is the common pineapple. With its rosette of long, slender, curving leaves, spiny along the edges, it is a thing of beauty. After

Bromeliad *Aechmea fasciata*

the fruit has been cut up to be eaten, simply place the green top in water to root. The first time I tried one, I was surprised to see roots sprout in a few days. Though not potted for four months, it was none the worse for its neglect. Plants require minimum care, and with patience you will be rewarded by the familiar fruits on tall, straight stems.

The bold, stiff, leathery leaves of bromeliads make them outstanding plants for modern interiors. On occasion, they will send forth spikes of colorful flowers to add to their appeal. Native to the tropical forests of the Americas, bromeliads grow, as do orchids, in decayed vegetable matter that collects in the crotches of trees. They are epiphytic, but not parasitic—that is they do not draw sustenance from trees, but merely use them for support.

Since they derive much of their sustenance from the air, bromeliads are also known as "air plants." A familiar example is the Spanish moss of southern gardens, a true bromeliad, known botanically as *Tillandsia*. The names of many bromeliads are unfamiliar, but are slowly becoming known. Some of these are cryptanthus, neoregelia, billbergia, vriesia, aechmea, puya, and dyckia. Most do not have common names, but the term "bromeliad" is commonly applied to all.

Coming from the tropics, these are warmth-loving plants, preferring the high sixty and seventy readings of the average home in winter. In their native environment, they receive filtered sunlight through the leafage of trees: hence they need only subdued light. They can be placed on coffee and other kinds of tables, on mantels and shelves, on sideboards and desks, and on wall brackets.

Bromeliads can be grown in the same osmunda fibre recommended for orchids. They will also thrive in a mixture comprised of equal parts leafmold, peatmoss, and sharp sand. Do not add fertilizer, and go light on feeding, except for light applications on pot-bound plants. In winter, keep them on the dry side. They can go for days and weeks without water, a reason they are recommended for the person with little time to devote to house plants. Many have funnel-shaped cups in the center of the rosettes of leaves; these cups should be kept filled with water, a feature that has given rise to their name of "living vase."

Queen's tears (*Billbergia nutans*) is an old-timer that seems to be protected by an armor, because it is virtually indestructible. Less known is *B. pyramidalis*, with olive-green leaves in the shape of a vase. Rose flowers with red bracts appear on the spikes. Cryptanthus are dramatic, with their rosettes of heavily marked leaves. *C. zonatus* has wavy-edged leaves, striped like a zebra. Small white flowers rise above the leaves, which are inclined to grow flat, like other cryptanthus. Form *C. z. zebrinus*, known as the zebra plant, is even more strongly marked.

A wide assortment exists among aechmeas. Living Vase (*Aechmea miniata discolor*) has slender, glossy green leaves, maroon underneath. Keep the cup in the center of its leaves filled with water at all times. Christmas Jewel (*A. racine*) has bright red, yellow and black flowers, while Finger of God (*A. orlandiana*) sports dark stripes on green leaves. Neoregelias also have colorfully marked leaves. The foot-long, metallic-green leaves of Fingernail Plant (*Neoregelia spectabilis*) are tipped with red. Crimson Cup (*N. farinosa*) has leaves that are narrow and bronzy-green.

Cast-Iron Plant

(*Aspidistra elatior*)

As maligned as this old-time Victorian parlor plant has been, I stand firmly behind it. If there is a sturdier plant, more able to take abuse (snake plant excepted), I would like to know what it is. For the person with a yen for living green under the most trying of circumstances, this is the answer to a dream. Aspidistra has long, arching, leathery dark green leaves, two and half feet long and three to four inches wide. Since these rise from the roots, there is no problem of legginess, and even large plants do not take up much space.

Once more becoming fashionable, this old-fashioned member of the lily family is also called barber shop plant. Small, one-inch-wide, bell-shaped, purplish-brown flowers, which appear singly, are seldom seen, because they develop close to the soil line. Two variegated kinds, with markings on their leaves, are more decorative. One is *A. e. punctata* with yellow-spotted leaves, the other *A. e. variegata* has leaves accented with greenish white stripes. Like all variegated plants, they can be used for accent and relief among solid-green-leaved kinds.

Cast-iron plant grows in any kind of soil, but responds to feeding and routine care. Divide every three to four years in the early spring, when the new leaves appear like spears at the base. Clean the foliage periodically to remove dust and to bring out the natural lustre. If variegated kinds are not overfed, their leaf colorings will be deeper. Aspidistras make good ground covers. in gardens in mild climates where they are hardy outdoors, luxuriating in the deep, cool shade of large trees such as the evergreen live oaks in the South in America.

Clivia

(Clivia miniata)

The common name of this spectacular member of the amaryllis family, native to Natal, is Kafir lily, yet it is usually simply called clivia. I first recall seeing it as a youngster at the Boston Spring Flower Shows. While others drooled over the acacias, my attention was captivated by the clivias, with their showy orange blossoms and sturdy, leathery, strap-like leaves. On my first trip to Europe, I was equally entranced by plants in dimly lit cafes and entranceways of apartment houses in Paris and Geneva.

Clivia resembles agapanthus, and requires the same care. Its shorter leaves, about a foot long and two inches wide, are symmetrically arranged, while those of agapanthus grow informally. Flowers usually appear in late winter and early spring. Stately stems support clusters of one to two dozens of three-inch lily blossoms. The overall effect is orange, but flowers are actually scarlet-orange on the outside and yellow on the inside. In a cool atmosphere, they last eight weeks or more.

Kafir lily thrives in an average soil. Plants can remain in the same containers for several years, since they like to be pot-bound, but they will require large pots or tubs as they increase in size. Individual bulbs can be planted in six-inch pots. Side shoots, taken from mother plants after they develop roots of their own, will make new plants.

Clivia enjoys cool temperatures in winter, in the forties or fifties if possible. Yet they do well in average room temperatures if soil is kept on the dry side in winter, the normal rest period. In early spring, give the plant more water and feed and provide sun to support new leaf and flower growth. Place it outdoors in summer in partial shade. *C. m. flava* is a yellow-flowering form.

Dracaena

(Dracaena)

With dracaenas you cannot go wrong. Tall growing, with slender, arching leaves on single stems, they are well suited to planters when

Dracaena marginata

combined with dumb canes, aglaonemas, ferns, philodendrons, and other foliage plants. Their one drawback is the tendency to lose their lower leaves as they grow taller. When tops are lopped off, the remaining stems will produce new shoots. Canes may also be cut into small pieces and planted horizontally in moist peatmoss and sand to make new plants.

The dracaena that is often propagated by the latter method is the Hawaiian Ti plant (*Cordyline terminalis*), a native of eastern Asia, with foot-long, spear-shaped, dark red leaves edged with magenta, and bright red leaf stems. At flower shows it is sold as "logs,"—pieces of stems coated with wax to prevent them from drying out. Planted in moist peatmoss or sand, they root and develop shoots.

Corn plant, one of the toughest of all house plants, usually appears in the form of *D. fragrans massangeana*, with broad yellow stripes along the centers of the arching leaves. Very slow growing, it does not generally lose its lower leaves, and can remain in the same pot for several years. *D. sanderiana* from the Congo is dainty, and has slender leaves, nine inches long and one and a half inches wide, accented with creamy-white margins.

Consider *D. deremensis* from Tropical Africa, with leaves that are two feet long and two inches wide, or its form, Warneck dracaena (*C. d. warnecki*), with white stripes along the narrow, shiny leaves. Tips are inclined to turn brown because of dry air or over- or underwatering. Among dracaenas, it is perhaps the trickiest. *D. gracilis* has long, narrow leaves, edged with maroon. Plants are slow growing, but as stems grow they develop a fascinating serpentine form. This is a good plant for hot dry apartments. *D. godseffiana* is one dracaena that looks more like a shrub, with heavily spotted, oval leaves on thin, wiry stems. Also a good keeper is the rare *D. goldieana*, with five-inch long leaves accented with zebra stripes that are gray and green. Give dracaenas basic care, but dust the leaves or wash them in the shower. Older plants will produce sprays of small white flowers, not showy but appealing in their way.

Dumb Cane

(*Dieffenbachia*)

Like dracaenas, these tall foliage plants, with broad leaves radiating on a single stem, certainly stand at the top of the list. The common name is derived from two characteristics. One is that the thick, juicy stems resemble canes. The other is that if one chews large enough portions of leaf or stem long enough, one is rendered speechless for a day or two. This, therefore, is a plant to keep away from young children who may have proclivities to sample greenery.

With their spotted and highly variegated leaves, dumb canes add pattern and "color" to groupings of house plants. Some are more decorated than others, like Rudolph Roehrs, with almost entirely creamy-white leaves, dark green along the midrib and the edges. New leaves are lighter in coloring, and nearly transparent.

There is no getting away from the fact that dieffenbachias tend toward legginess. Often plants shed a lower leaf every time they unfold a new one. The lanky habit is sometimes pictorial in particular groupings of foliage plants, as in large planters, where they add height and their nakedness is concealed by lower-growing plants.

Cut off tops from leggy plants and root in water, where the plants can be grown almost indefinitely. The rooted pieces, if you prefer, can be potted to make new plants. The remaining stub, or trunk, will send out new shoots. The stems can also be cut into small sections, three to five inches long, and placed horizontally in a medium of peatmoss and sand, where they will develop shoots. Tall plants can be air layered. (See Chapter 7.)

The most common dumb cane is *Dieffenbachia picta*, with leaves blotched with white. A native of Brazil, its varieties include *D. p. superba*, compact and creamy-green, and the already mentioned Rudolph Roehrs. *D. amoena* has huge leathery leaves that add a note of boldness to contemporary decors with their white markings on a dary green background. *D. seguine* comes from the West Indies, and has spotted leaves, pale green beneath, accented with prominent midribs. The leaves of its form *D. s. nobilis* are dull green, marbled with yellow-green. All produce small calla lily-like blossoms.

French Ivy

(*Fatshedera lizei*)

It was not too long after Second World War that I first became acquainted with French ivy, or tree ivy, as it is also known. I then thought it striking—and still do. This upright foliage plant, with three to five lobed star-shaped leaves, similar to those of English ivy but much larger, will eventually become several feet tall. Small plants stand up on their own and do not require support, but they need staking as they become taller.

Most often, French ivy is seen as a single-stemmed plant. It tends to lose its lower leaves, but side shoots appear on older plants. Pinch the tips and prune shoots constantly to stimulate branching. Interestingly, French ivy is a cross between plants of two genera of the aralia family, *Hedera helix hibernica*, a variety of the English ivy, and *Fatsia japonica moseri*, a form of the well-known evergreen shrub from Japan. The result is an excellent pot plant, with distinctive glossy leaves. Several stems are often grown in a single container.

French ivy makes a good plant for "decorative" exposures—for hall-ways and entranceways, for corners in living-rooms, for offices and banks. Dust the leaves occasionally to bring out the natural gloss. Placing pebbles or small stones on the surface of the soil enhances the overall appearance. The variegated form, with light green leaves marked with white, is slow growing. Like other variegated plants, it is more difficult to grow because the leaves lack chlorophyll.

Nephthytis

(Nephthytis)

This vigorous vine, in the same family as philodendron, is one of the most extraordinary of the clan. Best known is the common *Nephthytis afzeli*, with its, distinctly arrow-shaped leaves. It clings by way of aerial rootlets to the barks of trees in the tropics. I hardly know of a house plant that is easier to grow. It flourishes in the dimmest light, whatever its source. Fail to water and feed it, it nevertheless flourishes.

Syngonium Green Gold

Cuttings not only root easily in water, but thrive in water for long periods of time. Plants that are fed grow luxuriantly, and are certain to be the healthiest in your collection.

Similar in appearance and growth habit are the syngoniums. The nomenclature, in fact, is a confusing one, and the most widely grown of all, *Syngonium podophyllum* is now known as *Nephthytis afzeli*. All grow exuberantly and give off a sticky, milky juice when stems are cut.

Many variations are available, like the compact, crinkly-leaved Emerald Gem, the nearly white Ruth Fraser, Trileaf Wonder, and Green Gold, with leaves green-gold in the center and edged with green. The last is a variegated foliage plant that adds "color" to the indoor scene. I have been growing it for years, and would not be without it. All are dependable vining plants that can be trained on a piece of bark, a trellis, or stake, or grown in a hanging basket in front of a bright window.

Nephthytis responds to a rich, humusy soil mixture. An excellent foliage plant to grow in water, it is the arrow shape of the leaves that make it particularly appropriate in contemporary glass containers. Use them on dining-room sideboards or tables. Keep it in mind for the bathroom. Large plants can be grown in wooden buckets or large earthenware pots. Give plants a shower in the bathtub a few times a year to remove dust.

Palms

Like Boston fern and aspidistra, palms are durable plants from Victorian days that once again are gracing homes, hotels, and executive suites. Their durability is legend. With their gracefully arching, many parted leaves, they survive with little light and water. Because of their large size, they are primarily suited to large rooms, and are excellent for hotel and motel lobbies.

All palms are slow growing. They thrive in an average potting mixture, and can stay in the same containers for several years if they are fed with liquid fertilizer when they are actively growing. In summer, take them outdoors to partially shaded locations, since their leaves will scorch in hot, direct sunshine. The fronds of palms are notorious dust collectors. Wash them frequently with a moist cloth or, better still, give plants a shower in the bathtub.

Often used by florists to decorate weddings and banquet halls, fan palm (*Howea forsteriana*), native to the South Pacific, is one of the taller kinds, with spreading, graceful, airy leaves. Paradise palm and kentia palm are other common names. Popular in homes is the delicate

Fan and pygmy palms. On the table, a bromeliad *Vriesia speciosa*.

pygmy palm (*Phoenix roebeleni*), an elegant species from Burma. Small growing, it is noted for its fine, feathery leaves and graceful habit.

The Oriental lady palm (*Rhapis excelsa*) is a small kind, shrubby as it becomes older, with suckers along the base that cover the main stem, creating a bushy appearance. A slow grower, it has long, narrow leaves and stems thickly covered with hairs. Cocos or Weddell palm (*Syagrus weddelliana*) is outstandingly graceful, with a long trunk topped with fronds made up of narrow, shiny, bright green, finger-like sections. Tolerant of complete shade, it is often grown in a small tub as it becomes larger. It is hardy in gardens in Florida.

Unusual is the recently introduced erect *Chamaedorea erumpens* from Honduras—small growing, with fans composed of wide segments. Slender and compact, older plants produce suckers at the base that cover the main trunk. This palm adjusts to poor light, as well as air conditioning.

For many the most desirable is the truly diminutive *Neanthe bella* (*Collinia elegans*), a slow-growing species discovered in dry, shady forests in Yucatan, Mexico. It always stays small, only a few feet tall, and reaches maturity in a six-inch pot. Its dark green fronds are made up of thin leaf segments. The person who is a palm lover and lives in an apartment can grow this delightful member of the clan; it is so small, it seems toy-like.

Philodendrons

(*Philodendron*)

Among tropical foliage house plants, few have played a more significant role than the philodendron. For one thing, everybody knows it, and nearly everyone grows it or has in the past.

Philodendrons are popular because they are easy to grow in poor light under average home conditions. Available in many leaf forms and sizes, they particularly complement furnishings of modern decors.

Generally free of pests and diseases, philodendrons can dry out without harmful effects. Also disconcerting is the tendency of new leaves to grow smaller and smaller. This is due to insufficient light, and accounts for the failure of the new foliage of cut-leaved philodendron (*Monstera*) to split.

The word "philodendron" comes from the Greek, meaning "tree-loving." In their native tropical woodlands, these vines cling to the barks of trees by means of aerial rootlets to a great height in search of

Cut-leaved philodendron

light. Florists often train them on a piece of bark inserted in the pot. Yet some philodendrons are not vining, but self-heading—that is, their leaves develop from a central crown and have little or no stem. On the whole, these types take up less space, vertically if not horizontally.

Philodendrons do not require much light—one reason they make such good house plants. Yet leaves grow larger and greener in strong light. Too much direct sunlight burns or discolors the foliage. Sun in the early or late parts of the day, or sunlight diffused behind thin curtains, is usually best. In dim corners, supplement with artificial lighting and more so in winter. If possible, move the plants when they are making new growth to bright windows and replace them with others in your decorative scheme. Or leave them where they are, simply bringing in new plants when they become outworn. Cuttings can be rooted in water or moist sand to make new plants.

When repotting, use a rich soil, well supplied with humus. Philodendrons come from tropical jungles, where they grow almost entirely in decayed vegetable matter. Newly purchased plants can remain in the same container for two, three, or more years because the root systems are small. To repot, use soil made up of two parts leafmold or peatmoss, one part good garden soil, and one-half sand, dry manure, and crumbled charcoal to aid drainage. Scatter a sprinkling of a mixed fertilizer and bonemeal.

Philodendrons are moisture loving plants. Keep soil moist; overwatering is harmful, especially if pots stand in water. If stems of the heart-leaved philodendron rot at the base, it is due to diseased organisms in the soil. Unlike other philodendrons, the heart-leaved apparently requires a higher degree of humidity, and in a dry atmosphere will sometimes drop its leaves while they are still green. Chilling or low temperatures, lack of moisture, poor light, abrupt changes of environment from the greenhouse to the florist to homes—all these result in leaf dropping. Until it makes a good adjustment, it can be temperamental. Pothos, a similar plant with mottled leaves, is generally easier to grow because it is more tolerant of hot, dry air.

Philodendrons do not require much fertilizer, but should be included with other house plants in regular feeding programs. A high-nitrogen combination promotes larger, healthier leaf growth. It is normal for a certain percentage of the leaves to turn yellow and drop. This is apt to occur during dull winter months, but as stems become bare, cut tops off to root for new plants. Or combine the heart-leaved plant with large-leaved kinds to conceal their naked stems. Abnormal yellowing of leaves may be due to too much water (also causes brown spots on leaves), lack of nourishment, too little light, too much direct heat, or cold and drafty locations.

Floppy, leggy, elongated growth is caused by too little light; pinching and pruning make for compactness. Though it is not harmful to remove the aerial roots, it is better not to cut them off as they help to supply small amounts of oxygen. Most indoor gardeners prefer to leave them on because they are natural. Wash the leaves with a moist sponge or cloth to free pores of dust; use a mist atomizer frequently, and resort to showers in the bathtub occasionally to restore the natural gloss of the foliage. Commercial "leaf shines" may be used, though I think the resulting effect appears artificial and it is said to be dangerous if cats or other pets eat leaves treated with it.

Philodendrons can be kept compact, with leaves to the base, through frequent pinching. It is better to start with a new plant than with a leggy specimen. After deciding how long you would like the stems to be, pinch the tips. When new shoots appear at the upper nodes, remove them with the finger tips or a sharp knife or scissors. New shoots will develop, again most likely at the topmost nodes, but keep cutting them until others finally sprout at the base. Repeat the same procedure with new stems when they are long enough. This technique can also be practiced with other house plants.

Today's market is flooded with so many kinds of philodendrons that it makes for confusion. Some, like the proverbial heart-leaved (*Philodendron cordatum*), have small leaves a few inches long, while others develop leaves that, in the tropics, measure several feet across. New varieties are constantly being introduced. If you come across a kind you happen to like, just buy it.

Cut-leaved philodendron is sometimes listed as a *Philodendron*, but its true botanical name is *Monstera deliciosa*. It was also once classified as *Philodendron pertusum*. Other common names are Swiss cheese plant and ceriman. A native of Mexico and Central America, it is now a widespread outdoor plant in warm regions of the world. Large plants bear edible cone-shaped fruits. The equally popular *P. hastatum*, sometimes called the tobacco-leaved philodendron, has big, arrow-shaped leaves. Another large-leaved kind is *P. panduraeforme*, also called the horse's-head philodendron. Brought to this country by a G. I. from England after the Second World War, it has three-lobed, shiny leaves.

With its deeply cut leaves, *P. dubium* is an exotic beauty, a slow grower that becomes straggly after a while. *P. auritum* has three-parted leaves, and *P. pitteri*, recently introduced, displays heart-shaped leaves of enormous size. *P. squamiferum* from French Guiana is a charmer, and is also called anchor-leaf philodendron because of its leaf form. From Colombia comes *P. andraenum*, which is best grown in a greenhouse or conservatory because it likes humidity. Long, arrow-shaped leaves, often two and three feet long, are velvety irridescent, marked with ivory veinings.

Neat and compact is *P. gloriosum* from Equador and Colombia, with large, silvery-velvet, heart-shaped leaves and ivory bands radiating from the centers. For a touch of white, acquire *P. sodiroi*, a gem in the heart-leaved class, slate gray, with darker olive-green areas, silvery mottled in effect. Grow it in small containers to place on coffee tables. Self-heading philodendrons, which do not climb or trail, exhibit leaves that radiate from a central stem. One of the best known, *P. wendlandi*, is rugged and tolerant of dry air. Similar is *P. orlando*, though its leaves have short stems. *P. bipinnatifidum*, with deeply notched leaves, is similar to *P. dubium*, but is self-heading.

If you scan catalogs of large growers of philodendrons, you will be amazed by names you have never heard of : *P. quercifolium* from Brazil; *P. melanochrysum*; *P. krebsi* from Puerto Rico; *P. imbe*; *P. fenzli*; *P. bahiense* from Brazil; *P. varifolium* from Peru; *P. lacerum* from Jamaica; and many others, including choice hybrids. All are fun to collect, provided you have plenty of space indoors.

Pothos

(Scindapsus)

If there is one tropical foliage plant I would not do without, it is pothos. The most popular, called ivy-arum (S. aureus), closely resembles the heart-leaved philodendron with its glossy green leaves touched with yellow. Grown either as a climber, on a piece of bark or other support, or as a trailer in a hanging basket or on a wall bracket, I prefer it to philodendron, because its lighter green leaves are streaked with creamy-yellow.

Pothos is also easier to grow. It enjoys heat, but resents wetness, which causes stems to rot at the base. When purchasing new plants, make certain the stems have not started to rot at the soil line. Tolerant of small amounts of light, I have kept plants on a dining room sideboard, several feet away from windows, for more than three years, and replaced them only because I longed for fresh specimens. Pothos also grows easily in water.

The most common pothos, *S. aureus,* comes from the Solomon Islands, where it clings to the barks of trees, displaying heart-shaped leaves of enormous size, much larger than those of pot-grown plants. It has several attractive forms, like Silver Moon and Marble Queen, with white variegations instead of yellow. Pallid blotches on the leaves indicate that plants need more light. Equally handsome is *S. pictus,* a climber from the East Indies, with large, dark green leaves overlaid with silver. Usually trained as a climber, its variety *S. p. argyraeus* has green-silver markings.

All pothos grow well in a mixture of peatmoss and sand. They need heat and resent chilling. Pinch tips and cut back long shoots to stimulate branching.

Queen's Tears

(Billbergia nutans)

This member of the pineapple or bromeliad family deserves special mention. For toughness, it rates with aspidistra, snake plant, and corn plant. Among bromeliads, it is the most commonly grown and least expensive, a real old-timer, with a charm of its own.

Queen's tears, more usually called billbergia, has stiff, slender, gray-green, gracefully curving leaves, a foot and a half long, and one-half inch wide. Finely toothed, they form a thick cluster resembling a tuft of grass. Large specimens are often seen in small pots because they are so durable and require infrequent repotting. Drooping flower clusters, which account for the common name, are most unusual, as well as spectacular. The stems that arise from the center of the leaf rosettes support spikes with reddish-pink bracts and green and purple flowers, well supplied with yellow stamens, a color combination that is dramatic.

Billbergia will thrive in any kind of soil, though it will respond to a coarse mixture, with a plentiful supply of organic matter, as recommended for other bromeliads. It likes to be kept constantly moist, but needs sharp drainage. It can be grown in cool or warm temperatures and in poor light, making it just the plant for a cool, dim hallway or an odd corner of the living room. In spring, place outdoors in partial shade with other house plants.

The artistic person should not overlook queen's tears for the strong thrust of its linear leaves among the broad foliage of other tropical plants. Use it as a filler among large-leaved philodendrons, dracaenas, dumb canes, scheffleras, aglaonemas, rubber plants, and French ivies. Divide large specimens in the early spring. Or take suckers any time of the year for new plants to replace those that take up too much space.

Screw Pine

(Pandanus)

This is a plant with a distinctly tropical flavor, growing straight, with a single upright stem on young plants, spreading its long, arching, spiny leaves in spiral fashion—the reason for its common name, screw pine.

Since screw pine is extremely durable, it is often found in dimly lit corners of hotel lobbies and other public buildings, surviving where other delicate plants would succumb. There, too, it becomes a dust collector, because the sharp spines along the edges of the leaves make it difficult to clean. The technique is to run a moist sponge, cautiously, from the base of each leaf to its tip. Never travel in the opposite direction, as this would be against the spines.

Young plants are attractive, and take up little space. As they grow taller, they often become gawky. They also develop several suckers at the base. These will root easily to make new plants to replace the old, which may occupy too much space. As plants age, they also drop roots into the ground. Where hardy, they develop into sizable branching trees, and are often seen in gardens in Florida and other frost-free regions of the world.

Plants can remain in the same containers for many years, as they do not resent being root-bound. Eventually, however, they will require more root space. Use a regular potting mixture when transferring to larger containers. Feed screw pine sparingly, in spring and summer, with mild fertilizer applications, as too much food stimulates lush growth, which becomes soft in poor light. Plants do not resent drying out, which is one reason why they make excellent choices for hotels and business offices; they can be forgotten on week-ends and longer periods of time.

Most commonly grown is the green-and-white-striped *Pandanus veitchi*, with sharp spines along the edges of the leaves. It is native to Polynesia. *P. v. compacta* is a dwarf form, with pure white markings that tend to retain their coloring.

Also familiar is *P. utilis* from the island of Madagascar, where it attains sixty feet. Its dark green leaves, two to three inches long, are fortified with reddish-brown spines along the margins.

Less known are *P. pacificus* from the Pacific Islands, with short, broad, dark green leaves, and the spineless *P. baptisti*, with blue-green leaves, striped yellow in the center.

Also little grown is *P. sanderi*, characterized by green and gold bands. Its form *P. s. roehrsianus* has creamy-yellow stripes along the leaves. New foliage is a pleasant, soft, yellow-green.

Snake Plant

(*Sansevieria*)

The person who maintains that he cannot grow anything has certainly not given snake plant a try. With its erect, stiff, bold, sword-like leaves, emanating from thick rootstocks, it surmounts all kinds of adverse condition—poor light, dry air, heat or cold. Even pests and diseases seem to by-pass it, though it can be killed by overwatering.

The tall, slender, fleshy leaves of sansevieria are so familiar that plants hardly need description. The most common species is *Sansevieria trifasciata*, with dark green leaves, growing to three to four feet tall, marked and striped with subtle grayish-green. It is a slow grower, as are all sansevierias. More attractive is the variegated *S. t. laurenti*, with shorter, broader leaves, highlighted with horizontal markings of gray-green and edged with a wide border of golden-yellow.

Snake plants, with their upright, pointed leaves, have a streamlined appearance that makes them admirably suited to modern interiors. Especially outstanding is *S. cylindrica*, with long, thick, rounded leaves, marked with bands of light gray-green. On large plants, leaves may grow as tall as five feet. Some sansevierias are short and compact, with leaves that form symmetrical rosettes. One is the bird's nest snake plant (*S. trifasciata hahni*), with glossy leaves marked with gray bands on a background of light and dark green. Variants of this are touched with gold and silver. All remain low, ideal for coffee tables and narrow windowsills.

Sansevierias have other lesser known common names, among them bowstring hemp, lucky plant, and leopard lily. Lucky plant probably refers to the rugged, indestructible character of these members of the lily family that are native to Africa. Mottled leaf markings and spikes of small, sweet-scented, creamy-white flowers account for the name leopard lily. It is also called mother-in-law plant because its leaves resemble long tongues. Flowers develop on mature plants only.

If not overwatered, snake plants are extremely easy to grow. Water every week or ten days; plants can be neglected for several weeks, especially if kept cool. Use an average soil mixture, and feed during periods of active growth. Separate old clumps to make new plants. Or root three- to four-inch leaf cuttings in sand. Allow the pieces to dry for a day or two, and insert in sand in an upright position. Since cuttings of *S. t. laurenti* will revert to the green type, propagate this form by divisions.

As a group, sansevierias have been much maligned, perhaps because they tolerate much abuse. Yet their upthrusting leaves have a certain dramatic quality that denotes action—like exclamation points in large planters. I particularly like them in geometric containers—square, rectangular, hexagonal, or octagonal in form.

Grow Plants in Water

Indoor hydroponics makes it possible to grow plants in handsome containers that contribute to the decor of the rooms. The foliage plants that are grown in water need little light, natural or artificial. Even windows are packed with pot plants, there are still places—the table in the hallway, the bric-a-brac in the living room, the dresser in the bedroom—for plants that are grown in water.

Growing house plants in water is the easiest form of indoor gardening. Once set up, plants require hardly any care: add water as it evaporates, and occasionally apply a little highly diluted liquid fertilizer. Actually, water gardening is just the thing for busy people who work and take short or long trips frequently, since these plants can be left without care for several weeks. The types of containers to use depend on taste, but for the most part select solid colors, since decorated kinds may detract from the plants. Glass, ceramic, and plastic are suitable. Containers may be opaque or clear. My preference is clear glass in pastel colors, as I am fascinated by the network of roots, like the strong thrusting, coiling roots of Chinese evergreen and dumb canes and the fine roots of pick-a-back. I also like to see stems that criss-cross and the variety of roots when three or more kinds of plants are combined.

Tall containers will ususally support upright stems. Shallow receptacles will need pin holders, and these can be secured with clay, placed in position when the containers are dry. One or two stems inserted in the pin holder will brace and support stems of additional plants. If using sections from your own house plants, first root them in water and arrange them later, since some of the lower leaves may turn yellow before strong roots develop. If you decide to grow plants in water, knock off every bit of soil and wash the roots. In summer this can be done outdoors: in winter use the faucet, with a basin underneath. The latter method is used by apartment dwellers the year 'round.

Why is it that overwatering causes roots to rot, yet plants can be grown in water? A soil that is waterlogged shuts out air, and becomes stagnant and sour. But water itself contains air in sufficient amounts for roots to breathe properly. To help keep water clean and sweet, add charcoal, using a teaspoonful or two for each container. Finely ground charcoal is sold in small bags; when placed in water, it sinks to the bottom and is hardly noticeable. It lasts a long time, and can be reused whenever water is changed, once every month or two. As water evaporates, add more; use tepid or room temperature water kept in watering cans. Mist spray the leaves occasionally, but wash them thoroughly under the faucet when changing the water and cleaning the containers.

Feeding

Feed plants in water with mixed fertilizer, using a very weak concentrate in liquid form, since exposed roots, with no soil to protect them, burn easily. Keep removing yellow leaves, and cut back leggy growth on ivies, philodendrons, and other trailers. When dumb canes, aglaonemas, and other plants lose their lower leaves, cut off the tops and reroot in water. Though plants in water do not grow as well as those in soil, they do remarkably well. Yet after a while, six months or a year or two, they will need to be replaced with new plants. You can always use sections from your house plants when you prune or divide.

The kinds of house plants that can be grown in water are extensive. For bloom, rely on paper-white narcissus, an old-time favorite. Start bulbs in bowls or dishes with pebbles, stones, fibre or other medium that will support the bulbs. Add water up to base of bulbs, and place in a cool, dark spot for a week to ten days for roots to develop. Then bring them to sunny windows for flowering. I often start mine directly on window sills, especially as spring approaches. Results are equally good, and growth seems to be stockier.

Also grow the yellow, sweet-smelling Soleil d'Or and the Sacred Chinese Lily, white with orange centers. Both are tender narcissus that are more difficult to force than the paper-white, though much of the success is determined by the quality of the bulbs and how well they are ripened. It pays always to buy good stock. Fragrant hyacinths (insist on jumbo-sized bulbs) can also be forced in water in hyacinth jars if given a cool rooting period in the dark. Amaryllis are easier, and they too have flower buds already formed in the bulbs. They need only warmth, water, and light to develop them. Support the bulbs with stones or pebbles, with the water barely touching their base.

Water gardening is largely dependent on tropical foliage plants. The most familiar is the old-time Chinese evergreen (*Aglaonema simplex*), with glossy, dark green leaves. Hardly exciting, it is very dependable. The tops can be cut off and re-rooted when stems shed their bottom leaves. This occurs invariably as new leaves develop. Other aglaonemas include *A. robelini*, with large leaves variegated with silver. Grow dieffenbachias, commonly known as dumb canes, in water. One of the most striking is Rudolph Roehrs, with creamy-white leaves edged with green. There are many kinds of schismatoglottis that are similar in appearance.

Growing paper white narcissus in pebbles and water

Easy Kinds

Nephthytis of the same family is a top performer, a climber, with arrow-shaped leaves. Also grow the related syngoniums, with three-parted leaves often touched with gold. Do not overlook philodendrons of all kinds and the many versatile pothos, with heart-shaped leaves, including such varieties as Marble Queen and Silver Moon, with leaves streaked with white and gold. English ivies offer many possibilities, like the small-leaved Golddust and Maple Queen. Other good trailers are kangaroo and grape ivies. The tradescantias or wandering jews, called inch-plants, make outstanding hanging plants, and are often seen growing in water on desks in offices. Zebrina, setcreasea, with purple leaves, and flowering inch-plant (*T. blossfeldiana*) are less grown, but worthwhile.

Try pick-a-back, a mat-forming plant with maple-shaped leaves; snake plant (*Sansevieria*) for its thrusting, sword-like leaves; Sander's dracaena, with leaves striped with creamy-white; spathiphyllum, with arching leaves and white dove-like flowers; peperomias, with thick, shiny leaves; and umbrella plant or cyperus, a true aquatic often grown in fish aquariums. Try a dish garden, a shallow container, with many plants fastened to a pin holder, using Chinese evergreen, Sander's dracaena, snake plant for height, philodendron, and pothos, adding a few stones and pebbles to cover the holder. Many other interesting combinations are possible.

Avocado seeds will also develop into large-sized plants if they are suspended by toothpicks in water. Give sun or bright light.

Another way to brighten your house is to cut and use evergreen branches from the garden. Placed in water, they will remain in good condition for several weeks. Rhododendron lasts for months—and even flowers in water. Japanese yews, pieris, mountain laurel, leucothoe, mahonia, bull bay magnolia, pittosporum, podocarpus, pines (such as the exotic Japanese umbrella pine), cherry laurel, camellia, Japanese privet, and others can be "pruned" and shaped for this purpose all winter long. If you live in an apartment and do not have any evergreens in your garden, you can get them at florists at minimum cost—"lemon" leaves, "huckleberry," arborvitae, rhododendron, pittosporum, croton, camellia, yew, pine, false-cypress, podocarpus, and many others are usually available.

PART II

Ways and Means with Plants

(6)

House Plant Care

We hear much about the importance of soil, and rightly so. It is the medium in which plants grow. When it comes to building a house, emphasis is placed on a sturdy foundation. With the garden it is proper soil preparation that creates a sturdy foundation. House plants demand even more careful soil preparation because they must get along on abnormal conditions of light, heat, and air, plus a limited root run.

To a great extent, success or failure with house plants can be traced to soil. Its consistency, its ability to retain moisture, its drainage, its fertility (and its acidity, for such plants as azaleas and camellias) are vital factors. Oddly enough, color plays a minor role; it is a popular misconception that dark soil is rich.

Many of us have worked with soil for years, yet actually give little thought to what it is, what it is made up of. Soil is comprised of minerals and organic matter that have been broken down into tiny particles by heat, cold, moisture, air, and other elements of weather and climate. It contains bacteria, fungi, and other microorganisms that function under conditions of warmth and heat; it also holds decomposing organic matter, both plant and animal. Soil contains air, which is essential to plant growth. If saturated with water, the air supply is decreased and for this reason plants fail in soil that is kept wet and soggy.

The best way to understand the soil requirements of house plants is to study their native habitats. Cacti grow in deserts, in sand, with minor traces of organic matter. Azaleas, on the other hand, thrive on forest floors which are rich in humus.

Most house plants are of tropical origin. Foliage types subsist on very little light, but need quantities of humus in their soil mixture, similar to that of their jungle environment. A 50–50 combination of leafmold and sand is excellent.

Actually, house plants are amazingly adaptable in matters of soil. More than 90 percent will grow in an ordinary mixture if they are fed from time to time. Since a house plant recently obtained from a florist is usually provided with a specially prepared soil mixture, it will prosper for several months. Leave it alone as long as it continues to grow well.

POTTING MIXTURES—A potting mixture is made up of several ingredients—soil, often referred to as good garden loam; sand for drainage (or another inert material, such as perlite or vermiculite); and organic matter to retain moisture and promote bacterial action—peat-moss, leafmold, sphagnum moss, or garden compost.

To these basic ingredients fertilizer or plant food must be added—either a balanced commercial preparation or bonemeal or superphosphate, all of which are slow-acting phosphoric fertilizers. Adding crushed charcoal aids aeration and insures sharp drainage.

An easy way out nowadays is to buy commercially prepared soil, which has been sterilized to make it disease and weed free. In addition to the general potting mixture, special combinations are available for such plants as gardenias and camellias, which have a taste for acid soils, African violets and other gesneriads, geraniums, bromeliads, and cacti and succulents.

If you have a plentiful supply of garden soil, you may prefer to mix your own, especially if you grow a great many house plants. Apartment dwellers and those who grow a few plants may find it easier and more practical to purchase what they need.

A simple soil combination for most house plants includes two parts garden soil, one part leaf mold, peatmoss, or compost, and one part sand, perlite, or vermiculite. On this sprinkle enough bonemeal and a mixed fertilizer to whiten the surface. Mix all the constituents thoroughly with your hands or a trowel.

To prevent diseases and weeds, sterilize the soil mixture before adding the fertilizers by pouring boiling water over it or by baking in covered pans in the oven at 160°–190° F. for a half hour. Higher temperatures will destroy the organic matter in the soil. Allow the mixture to cool thoroughly before adding the fertilizers.

Tropical foliage plants, which come from hot, humid forests of South America, Africa, and Asia, are organic-matter hungry and need a mixture of equal parts loam and peatmoss or leaf mold, plus a sprink-

A contemporary plant room: camellia, lemon, philodendrons, Norfolk-Island-pine, fig.

ling of fertilizer. They can be grown in pure sphagnum moss if fed regularly with diluted fertilizer.

SPECIAL MATERIALS—Ordinary soil is too compact for air plants such as bromeliads and orchids, which like a light, fluffy, porous medium. Use osmunda fibre (the roots of osmunda ferns), which gives roots plenty of air, provides essential minerals for growth, and holds moisture in sufficient amounts. At the same time, it dries quickly enough to prevent roots from rotting. Orchid fir bark can be substituted. Use a mixture made up of six parts of either the osmunda fibre or the orchid fir bark and one part crushed charcoal.* Fill a third of the pot with crushed stones, broken pots, or other drainage material. If you do not have these materials, use equal parts of peatmoss or leafmold, sand, and charcoal.

It is equally important to sterilize pots in boiling water or to scrub them with a stiff brush in warm, soapy water. From time to time loosen the surface of the soil of pot plants with a kitchen fork or other small tool. Spread stones, marble chips, or pebbles on the soil of large plants to help conserve moisture, especially in summer when they are taken outdoors. Stone and pebble mulches are also ornamental.

Many indoor gardeners wonder about using beach sand in soil mixtures. Since it contains salt, it is definitely harmful. Washing the sand thoroughly several times will leach out the salt. But most salt-water beach sand is really too fine to use, so it is better to obtain coarse sand from a river, a pond or lake, or a bank along the roadside.

FREQUENCY OF WATERING—How often should you water house plants? Of all questions posed, this is the most difficult to answer in a few words, except to say: "It depends," followed by: "Water house plants when they need it—when soil surface is barely dry."

Questions pertaining to watering sometimes are more specific; "How often should I water African violets?" or "Should I water my philodendron once or twice a week?" There is *no* simple answer, because growing conditions vary: steam heat versus hot water heat; hot air heat versus convection or radiant heat: sunny windows versus shady. The best method is to feel the top of the soil with your finger tips. With a little experience, this practice becomes second nature. Dry soil is light in color—whitish, gray or buff. Moist soil is dark, black or grown; when touched, soil particles cling to finger tips.

Plants need water for several reasons, among them to dissolve fertilizer salts and transmit them as food to plant cells. Water keeps leaves and stems firm, and without sufficient amounts, plant parts lose their

*Osmunda fibre and orchid fir bark are sold at garden and plant supply shops.

turgidity. The evidences are often obvious: African violets, gloxinias, and shrimp plants droop; the leaves of wax begonias and inch-plants (*Tradescantia*) become shinier than is normal. They may droop and curl inward.

The kind of pot used plays an important part. Clay pots turn lighter in color when dry. When the sides are tapped with a spoon, they make a high, ringing sound, as opposed to deep vibrations of pots filled with moist soil. A pot plant that is dry, or nearly so, is also lighter in weight.

On the whole, it is advisable to allow the soil of most house plants to become slightly dry between waterings. Then soak the soil thoroughly, until water trickles through drainage holes. If possible, take your plants to the kitchen sink or the bathroom for these waterings.

House plants can be watered from above or below. Pouring water on to the top is the more usual method, but it may be placed in the saucer where it will be absorbed by the soil until the entire pot is well soaked. Both methods give satisfactory results, and a choice of one is largely a matter of preference. If a plant becomes bone dry, it is advisable to set the pot in a large basin of water and leave it there for an hour or more until the soil is saturated and no bubbles rise from it. When watering from below, be certain to dump out the excess from the saucer. If the surface of the soil is well moistened, this indicates that the plant has had enough.

Both too much and too little water are injurious to house plants. Allowed to dry too often, leaves turn yellow or brown along the edges —common symptoms that may not show up until later. Some plants, such as wax begonias and coleus, are very sensitive to drying out; others, like philodendrons, dracaenas, and scheffleras, are less so. Snake plant and aspidistra are hardly affected at all.

DRYNESS HARMS ROOTS— Plants with fine, delicate, fibrous root systems, such as African violets, wax begonias, coleus, and blood-leaf (*Iresine*), are easily damaged if allowed to dry out. Those with coarse roots and succulent leaves fare better—cacti, Christmas cactus, and epiphyllums, which show little or no injury to leaf tissues. Some house plants with woody stems, notably azaleas and gardenias, suffer from frequent drying out because their roots are very fine. Tips of branches that contain small amounts of sap wilt, turn brown, and die.

Wet, soggy soil causes considerable damage, and more house plants are killed by overwatering (often termed "too much kindness") than by any other environmental condition. Wet soil turns sour and shuts out air and eventually causes root rotting. Always remove excess water from saucers. Better still, rest the pots on a layer of gravel, pebbles, crushed stone, or turkey grits to catch the surplus. Make certain that the bases of the pots do not touch the water. Always remove water from jardinieres, which is easily overlooked because it is not visible. If pot plants are watered with care, with just enough to keep soil evenly moist, little or no water will pass through the drainage openings.

Water in the early morning rather than late in the day or evening. Leaves transpire and use up the water more quickly in the sun and in higher daytime temperatures. Remember that clay pots dry out much faster than plastic. Plants in containers without drainage holes generally need watering only once every week to ten days. When potting, use a thick layer of crocks, pebbles, or other drainage material, about one-third the depth of the pot, to catch the surplus. To water shallow Japanese dish gardens, immerse them in a pan of water and allow them to remain there until all air bubbles disappear.

Plants in cool conservatories and plant rooms with temperatures in the forties or fifties need water about once or twice a week. Plants in sunny windows require water frequently in clear, bright weather and less during dull, cloudy days. Proximity to radiators, registers, heat boards, and other sources of heat is a factor that influences watering. Plants on window sills or close to window panes receive the most sun, yet stay cooler on cold winter nights. Those in rich humusy soil and in large pots remain moist longer, while any that are pot-bound dry out faster. Flowering plants, like azaleas and hydrangeas, and those growing vigorously, demand more water.

PLANTS NEED TO REST—When plants are resting or dormant, gradually withdraw water. If they are kept cool in winter, they will need very little water. Blue lily of the Nile (*Agapanthus*), clivia, oleander, sweet bay (*Laurus nobilis*), bird-of-paradise, and orchid cacti (*Epiphyllum*), when they are resting, require very little. Use tepid water from the faucet or a watering can instead of cold water because it is less shocking. Some indoor gardeners like to use rain water collected in a barrel. Though softer, it does not contain minerals, except for a little nitrogen, but it is rich in bacteria.

Is chlorinated water harmful to plants? Actually, it is rich in minerals, and the usual concentrations of chlorine, as it comes through faucets, is not harmful. Water that is safe for human consumption is safe for plants.

The best policy is to keep watering cans constantly filled with water. Always replenish after making the daily rounds. Water that attains room temperature is suited to all kinds of house plants, including warmth-loving African-violets and other gesneriads, which are sensitive to cold water. A watering can that is kept filled can be picked up instantly at any time of the day or evening to water a plant that is dry, and in warm rooms in winter, flowering plants like chrysanthemums and azaleas may require watering two or three times a day. And if water is allowed to stand for several hours, the chlorine will escape.

I am particular about watering cans, for I consider them objets d'art. Handsome copper, brass, or other metal watering cans cost more than plastic, but they add to the decor of rooms in which they are kept. Copper and brass do not rust. Ceramic watering cans are equally attractive, but are heavy, and they break easily, a point to keep in mind where there are children, dogs, and cats. Watering cans may be a solid color or decorated, but whatever your preference, select those with long spouts and large enough openings for water to flow freely.

Small watering cans can be placed as ornaments on tables, shelves, sideboards, or desks, while the larger ones may be kept on the floor. Two, three, or more will save many steps—and much time—if plants are scattered throughout several rooms.

Where possible, group your house plants according to water needs. For example, keep in separate windows or rooms those that need watering once a day and those that require it only once or twice a week. This is helpful for the person who waters your house plants when you go on vacation. Labels in pots, indicating which plants require watering and how often, is a system that works well with me.

SWELLINGS ON LEAVES—Sometimes you will be confronted with a plant difficulty called edema. This is not a disease. Symptoms are leaves with water-soaked spots that burst and turn brown and corky, a condition caused by too much moisture. Saturated leaves, unable to transpire rapidly, will develop swellings.

Sometimes, too, you may notice drops of moisture on the surface of furniture, though you did not spill any water. These are droplets of moisture that exude from the tips of leaves, a method some plants have of getting rid of excess moisture. It occurs often with chrysanthemums, and I once had a philodendron, a variety called Burgundy, that was a chronic offender. Wipe the droplets from furniture and remove them from the tips of the leaves into the palm of your hand or on a piece of cloth. And remember: too little water is better than too much.

HOW TEMPERATURE AFFECTS PLANTS—As with light, plants react strongly to temperature. Those that are native to the tropics need warmth and high humidity, though many are extremely adaptable. Plants from subtropical areas prefer cooler temperatures, especially when they are resting in winter. Cacti, from desert regions, tolerate extreme heat by day and sudden drops of temperature at night. Here we are concerned primarily with temperatures during the winter months; in summer they cannot be controlled, except by air conditioning.

The ideal range of temperature for most kinds of house plants is a maximum of 70° F. during the day and 55° F. at night. This, of course, cannot be achieved in the average home, except in plant rooms. Nevertheless, it is ideal for most flowering and foliage house plants. And you should remember that no matter what the temperature is by day, it should be lower at night. A drop of 10° F., makes for greater success. Outdoors, even in the tropics, nights are cooler. During the daylight, plants manufacture their own food and at night consume it in order to grow. Without the stimulus of temperature change, plants are less able to function properly. Lower night temperatures are equally beneficial to human beings. We sleep better, and the air is less apt to be dry.

Actually, our behavior pattern is antithetical. At night, when we sit to watch television we raise the thermostat. During the day when we go to work we lower the thermostat to save on heat. Fortunately, most house plants do well at the indoor winter temperatures that we require for comfort—except for a few, such as azaleas, camellias, and Dutch bulbs.

The response of plants to temperature can be as erratic as their response to light. Some fail to set flower buds; if they do, buds drop or do not open if temperature is too high or too low. Camellia flower buds will drop if nights are warmer than 65° F. Gardenia buds stand still if the temperature is too low. Poinsettias shed leaves and African violets stop flowering. High temperatures often produce small, puny flowers, as with fuchsias, one reason why they make poor house plants. In gardens, blossoms on pansies, violas, turberous begonias, nasturtium, and stock become smaller as weather becomes hotter.

Ventilation is important. Open windows at the top for air circulation when the sun is shining; plant rooms with several sunny windows become overheated, even on cold days. Avoid direct drafts; if necessary, move plants to other locations. Temperatures in winter may vary considerably within a room. Plants at south windows may become overheated at noon; at night, they may be chilled because of proximity to the panes or drafts.

AIR CONDITIONING—Though air conditioning controls temperature and brings in fresh air, it also has a drying effect. Plants are not harmed if they do not stand in the way of its drafts. Since air conditioning keeps our indoor temperatures lower than outdoors, plants often grow slowly in summer and are apt to spurt into growth in the fall when air conditioning is turned off.

Do not be too hasty in taking house plants outdoors in the spring.

A series of warm days early in the season can be followed by cool weather that causes setbacks. In the northern areas of the country, Memorial Day, May 30, is considered usually the safe time to set out tender annuals and to put house plants outdoors. And bring them indoors early, before the first frosts and central heating is applied, as this makes for an easier adjustment. For winter culture, house plants may be grouped according to temperature preferences—those that grow well in the high sixties and seventies and those that respond better to cooler readings, say from 50°–65° F.

Plants that tolerate daytime warmth are in the majority and include begonias, gardenias, poinsettias, African violets and other gesneriads, such as episcias, achimenes, kohlerias, gloxinias, smithianthas, and columneas. Anthuriums, crotons, fittonias, pileas, marantas, and pellionias need warmth, as do philodendrons, dumb canes, dracaenas, scheffleras, spathiphyllums, nephthytis, palms, alocasias, peperomias, snake plants, bromeliads, aralias, and pothos.

In cool plant rooms, grow camellias, azaleas, Chinese hibiscus, acacias, sweet bay, clivias, oleanders, geraniums, English ivies, osmanthus, Norfolk-island-pines, Japanese aucubas, ardisias, osmanthus, and star of Bethlehem (*Campanula isophylla*). Cacti and succulents tolerate hot, dry air, with a considerable temperature drop at night. As a group, they are much overlooked, and are excellent plants to grow in an overheated apartment.

PLANTS NEED NUTRIENTS—To the house plant enthusiast, few sights are more pathetic than a starving, pot-bound house plant. Like other living organisms, plants must be fed periodically. The kind of plant food, the proper amount, when and how applied, as well as the speed with which it can be absorbed from the soil, to a great extent, determine success.

Plants vary in their need for fertilizer. Some require constant periodic applications, others require only occasional feeding. They need varying amounts of such elements as nitrogen, phosphorus, and potash. Certain kinds of plants survive and thrive on lesser amounts of nutrients; some cacti, orchids, bromeliads, and epiphyllums, which grow in decayed organic matter in the crotches of trees, derive nourishment from bird droppings and falling leaves.

If you have placed cuttings of English ivy or wandering jew (*Tradescantia*) in water and forgotten them for months, except to add more water, you soon learned that plants can survive for long periods on water and air. Chinese evergreen and dumb canes are suited to this kind of culture.

Plants that are resting do not require feeding; it can, in fact, be harmful. The most common danger in this matter of fertilizing is overfeeding—either too much or too often. If *one* teaspoon of fertilizer is recommended, do not use *two*. If advised to feed once a month, do not do so twice. Experienced gardeners tend to use smaller amounts than manufacturers recommend and to feed more often.

There are no hard and fast rules when it comes to feeding house plants. If given the proper soil at potting time, a plant will remain healthy a long time. Symptoms of hunger are easily recognizable. Usually, lower leaves start to drop, and new growth, if any, is smaller than normal and lacks vigor. Flowering is sparse, and foliage becomes yellowish, indicating a deficiency of nitrogen, magnesium, or some other minor element. If in doubt, remove the plant from its pot and inspect the roots. A solid mass of roots with minimum soil surrounding them indicates that it is pot-bound.

KEEP SOIL MOIST—When feeding with dry or liquid fertilizers, it is vitally important that soil be well moistened. Without sufficient water, nutrients are insoluble and cannot be conducted through the roots and into the stems and leaves. And if fertilizer is applied to dry soil, leaves will wilt and turn brown, a condition known as "burning." It is particularly important that soil be wet before applying fertilizer in powder form. However, do not fertilize a water-logged plant until it has partially dried out. If soil is dry, first water the plants; then feed them, preferably a few hours later.

Fertilizers may be organic or inorganic. Organics include dried manures, such as cow or sheep, cottonseed meal, and tankage. They are slow acting and rarely, if ever, burn. Though their effect is long lasting, they need bacteria to put them into action; bacteria need warmth to function. Many gardeners prefer to use dried cow or other animal manures, though these give off an unpleasant odor for days. They can be added to the potting mixture or scattered on soil of established house plants, at the rate of a level teaspoon to a six-inch pot. Scratch the fertilizer into the surface of the soil and water well. You can also use manure water: one cup of dried manure dissolved in a gallon of water.

Azaleas, gardenias, camellias, and other acid-loving plants react satisfactorily to complete fertilizers containing organic nitrogen. Plants that thrive on high-nitrogen concentrates include philodendrons, ivies, ferns, dumb canes, and other foliage plants. Special foods are available for such plants as cacti, azaleas, and African violets.

Inorganic fertilizers are available in several forms: powder, liquid, and tablet. Usually the powder is applied to surface of moist soil at the rate of a quarter of a teaspoon to a five-inch pot. It can also be dissolved in water, and applied as a liquid. See the package for manufacturer's recommendations. Ready for immediate use, it is absorbed quickly by plant roots.

LIQUID FERTILIZERS—Use liquid fertilizer in place of one regular watering, saturating soil well. Follow manufacturer's directions for amounts or dilute more. Liquid fertilizers can be prepared beforehand and stored in containers with tight covers, to prevent evaporation and contamination, in a cool, dry place. Since they do not undergo chemical change, this practice is a time saver. Tablet forms of fertilizers are easy to use. With a pencil, make a hole along the side of the pot. Insert the tablet, cover it with soil, and then water well. Directions indicate the number of tablets, according to the size of the pot.

Recently, foliar fertilizers have come into widespread use. Applied to leaves in diluted liquid form, nutrients are absorbed and plants respond quickly. In a matter of two days, yellowish leaves turn green. Do not use foliar feeding exclusively, but as a supplement to soil feeding. In winter, house plants can be sprayed in the basement or bathtub and in summer outdoors along with garden plants. Epiphytes, such as orchids and bromeliads, are particularly responsive to foliar fertilizers.

The three major minerals that are required in varying quantities for good growth and health are indicated on packaged plant foods by the letters N, P, and P. Or they may be spelled out: Nitrogen, Phosphorus and Potash (Potassium) but always presented in that order. The figures on packages indicate the various formulae, showing the relationship of these three basic elements: 5-10-5 means that the formula has five parts of nitrogen to 10 parts of phosphorus and 5 parts of potash in the mixture. Whether the formula is presented in soluble powder form, in liquid or in tablets the end result is the same, governed by the basic formula, for all perform in the same way.

Nitrogen stimulates leaf and stem growth. Nitrogen-fed plants are lush-leaved, dark green in color. Too much nitrogen in the formula results in soft stems and bloom will be sacrificed to provide foliage. Geraniums are a good example of plants with a low-nitrogen requirement but all flowering plants should take a low-nitrogen formula. Therefore the first figure of the formula should be low. Nitrogen is an element that leaches out rapidly from pots, however, thus requiring replacement with each feeding.

Phosphorus is largely concerned with flowering and the development of fruits and seeds. It also makes for good root development, proper cell structure and hastening maturity and helping to harden stems. It is important to provide phosphorus for geraniums, bulbs and most other flowering plants. Thus, the second figure in the formula should be larger for such plants. Superphosphate and bonemeal also supply phosphorus.

Like phosphorus, potash helps to harden stems. Soils well provided with organic matter usually contain some. Potash makes for sturdy growth and renders plants more resistant to diseases. It aids in the assimilation of food.

Commercially offered foods, especially formulated for certain kinds of house plants vary considerably in their formulae, according to the needs of the plants. They may be 5-10-5, 5-8-7, 7-7-7, 10-5-5, 15-30-15, 12-6-6, 20-20-20, or others. Let us sum up: if you have a plant that is grown mainly for *foliage*, not flowers, use a high nitrogen fertilizer, one with the first figure larger than, or the same as, the others, as: 10-5-5 or 10-10-10. Since blossoming plants require more phosphorus, select a food with a high second number, as 5-10-5 for African violets or 5-8-7, as found in the special African violet formulae. For woody plants or those which must have sturdy stems plenty of potash is required to build structure and make them more resistant to diseases. For them select formulae with high third numbers, as 5-10-10 or 15-30-15.

MINOR TRACE ELEMENTS—In addition to these three elements, formulas for which are indicated on the packages as 5-10-5, 4-8-4, or some other combination, including 0-2-10 for plants that do not require nitrogen, so-called minor trace elements are also needed to round out plant growth. Good garden soils contain some of these. Most complete fertilizers include small amounts of magnesium, iron, copper, zinc, sodium, aluminum, boron, sulphur, sodium, manganese, silicon, and calcium—the last needed to neutralize acidity.

It is a good policy to feed your house plants with two or three different brands of fertilizers, as one kind sometimes supplies what the other does not. Nitrogen, phosphorus, and potash percentages vary, as do trace elements.

Too much feeding is harmful, and it is better to underfeed your house plants. An excess of plant foods builds up toxic salts in soils, causing injury to roots to the extent that they are unable to absorb nourishment. Soaking soil thoroughly several times helps to get rid of excessive amounts of salts. Obvious evidences of overfeeding are shown by leaves that turn yellow or brown at the edges. Flower buds likewise tend to blast.

Indoors, except at very bright, sunny windows, plants use up less food than outdoors, where more light and sunshine are available. Foliage plants used decoratively in poorly lit areas require only small amounts of fertilizer, since without sufficient light, they cannot manufacture as much starch and sugar.

When it comes to feeding house plants, remember:

1 - Do not overfeed.
2 - Follow directions closely.
3 - Feed only when soil is moist.

HUMIDITY INSURES SUCCESS—If you were to analyze the reasons for the success of a group of house plants, one factor would doubtless be high humidity. This is why house plants grow so well in summer, whether they remain indoors or are taken outside.

Perhaps you have noticed that healthy plants often appear in groups. Except for individual specimens of tough kinds, like snake plant, dracaena, or schefflera, used for decoration at an entrance hall or on the living-room floor, most house plants are concentrated at windows or in plant rooms. Grouped together, they help each other by giving off moisture, increasing the humidity content in the air. The greater the number of plants, the higher the humidity, and the better the growth.

Central heating in our homes makes air bone dry. It is bad for plants, and does not do us good either. It is harmful to our nasal and throat passages, and some medical authorities maintain that colds are less apt to spread among members of a household where humidifiers are present. Dry air is also injurious to furniture, fabrics, and especially antiques. Collectors know this, and resort to mechanical humidifiers to prevent furniture from drying out. Anyone who has worked in a museum knows that a humidity reading is taken daily. Temperature and amount of moisture in the atmosphere are correlated. The higher the temperature, the greater capacity of the atmosphere to support moisture.

Plant leaves are constantly giving off moisture. It transpires through the foliage, as well as the soil. It evaporates through the sides of the pots if they are porous, like clay. Plants also absorb moisture from the air. Giving them more water at their roots is not a substitute—the vapor must be in the surrounding atmosphere.

The amount of humidity determines how much moisture plants will lose through their leaves. The drier the air, the greater the loss. The higher the rate of transpiration, the more severe the injury to plants. Their stems and leaves become dehydrated, in spite of sufficient quantities of water in the soil. Stems lose their plumpness. Leaves begin to wilt and become pallid, yellowish, and brown around the edges, often dropping off. Sometimes leaves will drop while they are still entirely green, but this is caused by an abscission layer, which forms between the stem and petiole, shutting off nutrients from the leaf. It occurs frequently with heart-leaved philodendron, and is prevalent with plants that require high humidity, such as pellionia, aphelandra, and crossandra.

WHY BUDS BLAST—Low humidity results in new growth, with small, lifeless leaves, as seen on philodendrons in hotels, offices, and department stores. Flowering is scant, and if buds develop, they dry up and drop. Some may show color, but then blast—that is, fail to open. This happens frequently with gardenia and camellia, which require a high degree of humidity. (Gardenia, however, likes warmth and camellia needs coolness.) It occurs with gloxinia in winter. Humidity will be increased if you set pots on pebbles or crushed stone placed in saucers or trays, which are then filled with water. Watch the water level carefully, and add more as it evaporates, perhaps daily or two or three times a week. The layer of pebbles also holds the excess drainage water. As the water evaporates it benefits the plants directly.

Trays can be constructed to fit any window sill, even an oddly shaped bay window, or a top a radiator. But a radiator is not the best

Fern and spathiphyllum plants, resting on saucers filled with pebbles.

place for house plants, though many kinds grow in spite of excessive direct heat. Trays can be rested on the floor, where large low windows provide good light. A plumber, tinsmith or carpenter can construct trays of copper, zinc, or galvanized iron; you may have the facilities to make your own. Copper is the best material, as well as the most expensive; zinc is good and pliable, so that it can be worked easily.

Trays can also be shaped from aluminum sheets, purchased at a hardware store, which cut easily with strong scissors or tin snips and can be molded into shape with pliers and other tools. Though not handsome, such trays are inexpensive, and will last for years. Remember that trays will catch excess water, but are not intended for watering plants from the bottom; their purpose is to increase humidity.

Trays should be an inch or an inch-and-a-half deep in order to hold a thick later of pebbles, gravel, crushed stone, or sand. Turkey grits or pebbles are both excellent to use in containers to grow paper-white narcissus in. Zinc or galvanized iron trays can be given a coat of aluminum paint to make them more attractive.

In lieu of metal trays, consider custom-made planters. Constructed several inches deep to resemble window boxes, they can be rested on narrow or wide window sills, on radiators, on tables, on the floor, or on specially built stands. The purpose of the planter is to foster humidity; do not set plants directly in soil, but cover pots with moist peatmoss, perlite, vermiculite, or sand. Or rest them on a thick layer of pebbles or crushed stones, maintaining water at a safe level. There are advantages to keeping plants in pots—they can be turned around to keep them symmetrical, and they can be easily repotted or removed to be mist-sprayed, pruned, or fed.

PANS OF WATER—Another way to increase humidity is to keep pans or other receptacles filled with water on or near radiators or in corners of rooms. Available is a slender specially constructed metal container that can be suspended by hooks on the back of a radiator. If houses lack radiators, large, attractive, water-filled containers, like old-fashioned jardinieres, can be placed in rooms where plants are kept. New houses are often heated by hot air furnaces with humidifying devices. If you are fortunate enough to have one, make sure it works properly.

To supplement these devices use mist sprayers or atomizers on your house plants regularly. The so-called fog type, with a very fine mist, is highly recommended. Though it hardly seems to "wet" the foliage, droplets of water collect after a while. Many types of mist atomizers are available, including copper, which is sturdy and attractive and does a good job. Whether you choose this kind, or the inexpensive plastic, keep the mist gun handy, close to plants. It will remind you to pick it up and use it in spare moments.

Unless you have used mist atomizers before, you will find them deceptive—in the sense that they "wet" the surrounding areas more than you think. This is not harmful to plant stands or old furniture, but a new, highly polished table or a sideboard can be stained easily. Place a heavy cardboard in the back of plants when you mist spray. I set my plants in the middle of the living room rug or on the bathroom floor, allow them to dry completely before returning them to their permanent places. Aerosol bombs to control insects can be used in the same way.

It is often tedious to use a mist sprayer daily or several times a week. Another method is to carry plants to the kitchen sink once a week to syringe the foliage or wash the leaves under a gentle flow of warm water from the faucet. After washing, allow them to dry in the shade. The foliage of some plants, like the hairy leaves of African violets and other gesneriads, will scorch if dried in the hot sun. Use the bathroom to give plants a tepid shower once or twice a week. It removes dust and revives limp leaves. When washing them, rest pots on their sides to avoid oversoaking and spattering of soil. Always use a gentle flow of warm water.

USE HUMIDIFIERS—If possible, use mechanical humidifiers. These operate electrically, are controlled by a humidstat, and do not make noise. Moisture that vaporizes does not collect on furniture. Humidifiers use an astounding amount of water. An advertisement I saw recently described a console humidifier with an automatic humidstat, a visual water-level indicator, a ten-gallon rustproof tank, and a humidity output of fifteen gallons daily. Humidifiers are a worthwhile investment for plants, home, and health.

Fortunately many foliage plants from the tropics, where humidity is high, will adapt to dry air, among them aralias, scheffleras, French ivies, hoyas, philodendrons, pothos, rubber plants, and dracaenas. This is because they have smooth, glossy, hard-surfaced leaves that give off little water. What happens when plants are overhumidified? Such a situation will promote fungus diseases. Cacti, aloes, succulents, crassulas, and other plants from dry regions of the world become soft and tender.

Ventilation and humidity are closely interwoven. Some experts maintain that house plants need fresh air, others that they do not. I would say both are right, and in my reading I have found both points of view well substantiated. I have grown house plants successfully according to both theories, without noting any difference. Drafts, however, are harmful, and some plants, like poinsettia, are more susceptible than others. Always keep plants away from doors that are opened constantly, particularly in winter when air is cold. When plants become chilled, their leaves turn yellow and drop.

Fresh air does increase the humidity content in the home. During "warm" days in winter, open windows, from the top if possible (since hot air rises). Avoid cold drafts. Remember that tropical plants are sensitive to chilling.

Some plants native to temperate climates are tolerant of cooling breezes, among them pick-a-back, pittosporum, Japanese aucuba, sweet bay (*Laurus nobilis*), primrose, podocarpus, Japanese privet, oxalis, and geranium. But on very cold nights draw the shades or draperies, or place several thicknesses of newspaper or heavy cardboard between the panes of glass and the plants.

REPOTTING TECHNIQUES—When do house plants require repotting? What are the "symptoms" to look for? Every inexperienced gardener has to learn when a house plant needs repotting. Yellowing foliage, drooping appearance, stunted growth, failure to bloom, and a too small pot in relation to top growth are all telltale evidences. Yet the fact that house plants are doing poorly does not always mean repotting is in order. Inadequate drainage, over-or underwatering, starvation, insufficient light, or insects might well be the trouble.

The surest way to determine whether a house plant needs repotting is to remove it from its pot and examine its root system. If you see a solid, intricate, and impenetrable network of roots, with little loose soil, repot immediately. A plant can be shifted any time it needs it, if handled with care; but two periods are best—late winter to early spring, and fall.

I prefer February and March, because this is the end of the dormant period for most plants. New growth, triggered by increased amounts of daylight and more intense sunshine, starts to develop. It is the time when African violets and geraniums flower more freely, and new shoots expand on philodendrons, ivies, and begonias. Clivias, hoyas, Christmas cactus, epiphyllums, dracaenas, palms, prayer plants, Chinese hibiscus, crassulas, oranges and lemons, aralias, scheffleras, and others break their dormancy at this time.

Fall is also appropriate, but primarily for plants that outgrew their containers in summer or those that were overlooked in spring. Some fast growers, particularly in junevile form, benefit from repotting twice a year.

If you have a basement with a potting bench, consider yourself lucky, particularly if you have many plants. You can also use a spare room or the kitchen table covered with newspapers. In warm weather, you can repot outdoors on the porch, terrace, or driveway. Repotting is a messy job that requires a variety of supplies.

HOW TO REPOT—To remove a plant from its pot, turn it upside down, placing the fingers of the left hand around the stem to prevent the soil from falling out. To get a firmer control, press the stem between the first and second fingers. With the right hand, grab the edge of the pot and tap the rim on the edge of a table, bench, or kitchen sink. Be firm, but gentle. After one or more persistent taps, the ball of soil should come out intact. Sometimes it will not, usually because thickly matted roots adhere to the sides of the pot. In that case, insert a kitchen knife and run it around the pot between the soil and side of the pot. This will injure some of the roots, but will do no real harm, and it will loosen the ball of earth.

Occasionally, you will have to remove a plant by pulling it forcibly by its stem. Such woody plants as camellias, scheffleras, and ficus, and such "toughies" as snake plant, can be tugged while hitting the pot on its rim or side. Valuable containers will not break if you tap them on a thick blanket, but always proceed with care to avoid chipping or breakage.

When neither tapping nor knife insertion gives the desired results, resort to breaking the pot with a hammer if it is not a valuable one. With plastic and common clay pots there is no great loss, and the

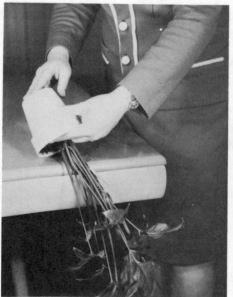

Tapping the pot on the edge Removing the ball of soil around the roots.
of a table, to loosen soil.

Pressing the fresh soil around the root-ball.

broken pieces of clay, called shards, can be saved for drainage material when potting.

Before removing plants to examine their roots, be sure the soil is moist. The ball will come out easier, and the soil is less apt to fall apart. Both very dry and wet soils may crumble and break apart; this is particularly true if the plants have small root systems. Before removing a plant from its pot, touch the soil with your finger tips. If it is dry, water the plant and allow a few hours for excess water to drain off. Then the soil will be moist, spongy, and adherent.

The general rule in repotting is to shift the plant to a pot one size larger, that is, a half-inch or an inch wider across the top of the pot. With fast-growing plants, skip one or more sizes, but remember that overpotting can be harmful to some plants. It is better to use a small size; if the pot is too large, the soil stays wet and soggy.

DRAINAGE MATERIALS—To pot: first, soak clay pots in water (glazed or ceramic pots need only be washed), then place a piece of broken pot, called a shard or a crock, over the drainage hole of the new pot, with the concave side down. Cover with a one-half to one-inch layer of flowerpot chips (clay pots crushed into tiny pieces), gravel, large pebbles, coarse compost, flaky leafmold, small pieces of charcoal, or sphagnum moss to prevent soil from washing through drainage opening. You may have noted that professional growers often fail to do this. One reason is to save materials and labor. They also use a very light, fluffy soil mixture, which is not packed tightly. Then, too, they often deal with plants in tiny pots, which are sold quickly and are to be repotted soon after the buyers take them home. In any case, do not follow their example. They are experts, and know many little tricks. Besides they raise their plants under ideal conditions.

Next add a layer of potting soil over the drainage material, a half-inch or an inch or two, depending on the size of the pot and the root-ball. Loosen and remove, with your finger tips, all crocks or other drainage material enmeshed in the roots at the base of the ball of earth. No doubt some roots will be broken, but healthy plants will not suffer much setback. With your left hand, hold the plant in position, so that the new soil surface will be a half-inch to an inch below the rim of the new pot. With your right hand, insert fresh soil around the root-ball, and press with your fingers, to bring the soil in contact with the roots. This eliminates air and steadies the plant. For small pots, firm the soil around the edges with the blunt end of a pencil or a wooden plant label. With larger pots use an inch-wide garden stake. Whatever its size, this device is known as a "potting stick."

FIRM BUT GENTLE—Next press soil firmly but gently so as not to break the roots or pack the soil so tightly that water will not drain through easily. For these reasons some experts believe it is better not to tamp at all, but moderation is the best approach. Until the desired level is reached, keep adding soil, pressing again with the fingers, tapping the bottom of each pot on the surface of the work bench or table so that the soil will settle around the roots. Make certain that the plant is centered and that the base is not placed too deep or too high. The space at the top of the pot is needed to hold water, and many indoor gardeners know how exasperating it is to water a plant when the soil is nearly even with the rim. Such a plant may have to be watered several times a day, and even then not receive enough moisture to take care of its needs.

When finished, water each plant thoroughly. Two or three applications may be needed, depending on pot size. If clay pots were not soaked beforehand (this is advisable), they will absorb most of the first application. After these first waterings, do not water again until the soil is slightly dry. If the roots were disrupted in repotting and sections of the soil fell apart, keep the plants in the shade for several days or a week or more to recover.

Not all plants require repotting. This is particularly true of large specimens—oleanders, camellias, azaleas, clivias, cut-leaved philodendrons, ficus, and jade plants. Simply remove soil from the top of the pot and replace it with a fresh mixture containing fertilizer. You can do the same with small containers if your space for house plants is limited. Though some of the surface roots are cut when soil is removed, this is not usually harmful to healthy plants.

ALTERNATE METHOD—If you do not have time to repot, especially if plants were repotted the previous year, merely topdress them; that is, sprinkle mixed fertilizer on the surface according to recommendations on the package, and work it in with a fork, small stick, or other tool. This will perk plants up considerably, and keep them healthy for several months or even a year. Many prefer this method, but when pots are packed with roots, you will do better to repot.

Another method, if you cannot afford space for larger containers, is to remove plants, break some soil away from the top and sides, and repot in the same container with fresh soil filled in around them. Generally, it is best to know which plants are suited to this rough handling. Some, like snake plant, aspidistra, chlorophytum, Moses-on-a-raft, and queen's tears (*Billbergia nutans*), are practically indestructible. If many roots are cut by using this method, it is a good practice to reduce some of the top growth by pruning.

Plants in very large pots that have been damaged by excessive watering can be salvaged if they are transferred to smaller containers. After removing the plant from the container, shake away all the soil from the roots, and cut off rotted portions of root. If the plant then seems to be worth saving, repot it into a smaller pot, using light, well-drained soil—equal parts garden soil, sand, and peatmoss or leafmold (preferably sifted). Keep the plant out of the sun and water it lightly until it shows signs of recovering. To lessen transpiration, cut off some of the top growth.

With seedlings the potting procedure is different. Fill the pot with soil nearly to the top. Make a hole with your fingers, a small spoon, or stick, and insert the seedling, pressing it gently into the soil. Water thoroughly. Seedlings that are growing rapidly will need transplanting frequently, depending largely on the kind of plant. Follow this same procedure with small rooted cuttings of geraniums, coleus, African violets, ivies, tradescantias, and begonias.

141

The Vacation Dilemma

When you grow house plants, you are faced with the problem of what to do with them when you take a vacation. This involves the long annual vacation in the summer or the winter, as well as shorter trips. For the week-end, plants that dry out quickly can simply be soaked thoroughly and placed in shade.

If you take frequent trips, rely on cacti and succulents and on resilient foliage plants, such as philodendrons, pothos, dracaenas, and snake plants, which can go without water for ten days or longer, depending on the room temperature. Plants in plastic pots stay moist longer than those in clay pots.

A dependable relative, friend, or neighbor can look after your plants. If he or she is an experienced gardener, you will return to find them in excellent condition, but with the inexperienced anything can happen. Plants will be either too dry or too wet. No matter how explicit your directions, they are often misinterpreted or not followed at all.

SHORT VACATIONS—Before leaving for a vacation, soak all plants thoroughly. Take them to the kitchen sink or bathtub or place pots in basins of water. Do not wait until your departure day, but do this the day before you leave. Remove plants from direct sunlight to shady locations, where light is strong, as in north windows. Or draw shades or adjust Venetian blinds, making certain plants are not near radiators, blowers, or other heat sources. In winter, lower the thermostat, since soil stays moist longer in lower temperatures and water transpires from foliage at a lower rate.

Another aid is to cover pots and plants entirely with transparent polyethylene plastic, such as food bags available at food stores. Insert the pot in a plastic bag, wrap it around the stem or base of the plant, and tie the loose end of the bag with string or wire. For large pots, use sheets of plastic. Small plants that tend to dry out quickly can also be covered with plastic bags placed over the tops, with the ends tucked under the pots. For large plants use sheets of plastic, secured at the base.

The plastic sheet acts as a miniature greenhouse that keeps in humidity, while allowing the foliage to breathe. Groups of house plants can even be placed on tables and covered with large pieces of plastic, such as those used to cover clothes by dry cleaners. Tuck the ends under the pots and insert stakes in several of the pots to prevent the plastic from resting on the tops of the plants. Keep plants in the shade; in sun, plastic heats and causes burning.

If you vacation in summer and have a garden outdoors plunge pots

Plants covered with plastic, for vacation or to hasten rooting cuttings.

Ferns and philodendrons, outside for the summer.

up to their rims in the ground. Select a shady location, for even the sun loving plants, and soak thoroughly with water, including the area around the pots. Then mulch with shredded bark or wood chips. Plants will stay moist for as long as two weeks, particularly if it rains. Another method is to place pots in bushel baskets or boxes and cover the pots with moist peatmoss or soil after soaking. Keep in the shade of a building or a large tree. If you have only a few plants, you can ship them to a friend's house or garden, where they will be looked after while you are gone.

VACATION OUTDOORS—An entire summer vacation outdoors does house plants a world of good, a practice that is recommended wherever this is possible. Whether placed in the garden, on porches or terraces, or on city balconies and fire escapes, plants grow quickly and revive during the long, warm days of summer in the great outdoors. When taken indoors in the autumn, they are hard to recognize and look like greenhouse specimens that would win blue ribbons at flower shows.

The time to take house plants outdoors is after warm weather arrives and all danger of frost is over. It is better to be late than too early. A few warm days in spring can be beguiling, but be cautious; the chilling that often follows damages tender leaves; unexpected late frosts are more harmful, causing setbacks that require weeks to recover.

To get house plants ready for vacation time, first discard any that have outlived their usefulness. Cut back leggy specimens and take cuttings for new plants. Repot any that have been overlooked, but avoid oversized pots. Do not place house plants in hot, direct sunshine immediately; adjust them to their outdoor environment gradually, moving them from shade to partial shade to sun. Even plants from the sunniest windows may scorch in the strong sun of spring and early summer.

For most kinds (except cacti and definite sun lovers), a partially shaded location is ideal. Sunshine a few hours a day, early or late, or as it filters through the branches of trees, suffices. The north sides of structures are excellent. Lath screens or houses are perfect for orchids, bromeliads, begonias, and just about all kinds of house plants, as they subdue sunshine and break the force of the wind. Geraniums, cacti, crown-of-thorns and other succulents, epiphyllums, palms, azaleas, camellias, tender euonymus, holly osmanthus, orange and lemon trees, and shrimp plant are some that benefit from sun several hours a day; foliage types, such as philodendrons and scheffleras, prefer partial or complete shade.

If possible, plunge the pots in the open ground up to their rims where plants are sheltered from strong, drying winds. Pots in the ground are well anchored and draw moisture from the surrounding

Fiddle-leaved rubber plants, in pots plunged in ground for the summer.

soil, so do not dry out as often. They also benefit from rain and can be watered with garden plants.

To set a pot in the ground, dig a hole larger than the container, as well as deeper. Place a two-inch layer of broken pots or gravel at the bottom for drainage and to prevent roots from growing through the pot drain openings. Large holes can also be dug to hold several small pots. Firm the areas about the containers with soil, using your hands or a trowel and make certain that the rims are an inch or two above the soil level. If they are completely covered with soil, roots will grow over the rims.

Care for houseplants in the summer is routine. Water regularly, and do not depend on rain; those under trees or shrubs or close to structures, as under eaves, hardly benefit from summer showers. Feed every two weeks, since plants are growing rapidly in summer, and spray occasionally with a foliar fertilizer, but only as a supplement to root feeding. Whether pots are in the ground or on a hard surface, turn regularly to maintain symmetrical growth. Pinch and prune and stake. And check for pests; mealy bugs, scale, and red spider mites, difficult to eradicate indoors, are more easily controlled outdoors.

Some gardeners like to remove the plants from their pots and wet them in the open ground to give them free root run. The disadvantage is that roots must be cut and plants will receive a shock when they are lifted and potted in the fall; in spite of great caution, soil often falls apart, particularly with larger specimens. It is another matter, of course, to plant cuttings of houseplants such as wax begonias and Swedish ivy, in borders to fill bare spots, treating them instead as annuals.

BRING INDOORS EARLY—Start to think about bringing houseplants indoors early. The precise time varies with the part of the country usually around September 5 in the North, but it is better to be too early than too late. Most house plants, native to the tropical regions of the world, are susceptibele to chilling.

The purpose is to avoid early frosts and to get plants indoors a few weeks before central heating is turned on so they can make an easier adjustment. Air outdoors is humid and temperatures drop at night, while indoors the atmosphere is dry and temperatures are constant; more often the thermostat is raised at night. This is contrary to the natural needs of plants, which require less heat at night when the food manufacturing processes stop.

Open the windows after houseplants are brought indoors to make the transfer more gradual. Some leaves will turn yellow, but after a while this will cease on healthy plants.

As a rule, the indoor trek is not accomplished at one time. First, gather plants in one spot: the porch, terrace, driveway, or under a tree. Wash foliage with a hose or watering can and clean pots with moist cloth or sponge; clay pots may need scrubbing. Some plants will need repotting; most will benefit from pruning. Cut back extra long shoots, remove dead growth, pinch tips, and stake as needed.

Even if you have been feeding your plants all summer, feed them again with liquid fertilizer, or scratch into the surface of the soil bonemeal or an organic fertilizer, such as dry manure. Spray with an all-purpose combination as a precautionary measure, since house plants invariably bring pests and diseases with them, though you may not suspect it. The task is more easily done outdoors than in.

Plants set in the open ground should be repotted early. Lift carefully with a moist ball of earth, using a sharp trowel or small shovel for larger plants. No matter how carefully done, this operation is shocking to plants. Keep them in shade, water often, and bring indoors a week or two later.

Small shapely geraniums, wax begonias, patience plants, coleus, and other plants can be potted, as well as a few annuals—sweet alyssum, ageratum, dwarf marigold, lobelia—for sunny windows. Pot up parsley, mint, sweet basil, chives and other herbs for sunny kitchen windows.   Before bringing your house plants indoors, wash window sills, tables, stands, planters, and accessories such as saucers and jardinieres. Attach to window frames a few hanging baskets for English and Swedish ivy, zebrina, and episcia. And have a carpenter build trays over radiators or on window sills, if you have not done so before.

(7)

New Plants from Old

Once you acquire a handful of house plants, you begin to wonder about another aspect of plant culture: propagation. Increasing house plants is often a matter of necessity. When nephthytis, snake plants, dumb canes, or rubber plants become too large, you want small ones to take their place. Sometimes you would like to have young, rooted plants to give to friends or to contribute to a church fair or another community project. Propagating house plants is fun. Tremendous satisfaction comes from rooting and growing your own pot plants from cuttings, just as there is in making a dress, baking a cake, building a fence or a cabinet. Many indoor gardeners consider it the most stimulating aspect of growing plants.

House plants can be propagated at any time of year. Cuttings of ivies or geraniums or the tops of leggy dumb canes can be inserted in water in April or in December. So, too, plantlets from strawberry begonias or spider plants can be rooted in light soil, and a pot-bound snake plant may be separated into small sections, whenever you wish.

In spring, when increased daylight stirs cells into action, rooting is generally quicker and better. Start to propagate just before new growth comes in, avoiding, as a rule, the dormant period of winter. After flowering has ceased is also a "natural" time for propagating.

The easiest method of propagation is known as division. This consists of taking plants out of their pots and separating them into sections of varying sizes, each with strong root systems. With proper care, young plants will succeed because they are already well supplied with roots. Some plants can be divided by hand, others must be separated

Rooting plants in water: a cut pineapple top.   Zebrina cuttings

Rooting geraniums: cutting the stem.   The newly rooted cutting, ready for planting.

with a knife, a spade, or pruning shears. Aspidistra, snake plant, spa-thiphyllum, chlorophytum, African violet, prayer plant, and Boston fern are a few that can be handled this way. Divisions can also be taken by cutting with a knife vertically, without removing the mother plant from the pot.

Using cuttings is a more familiar method. New plants can be made from pieces of stems two to four inches long, from pieces of roots, or from an individual leaf with a portion of stem attached. Placed in water, sand, or light soil these cuttings will form roots. Rooting time varies with the kind of plant. Opaque containers will hasten rooting in water because they exclude light. Begonias, geraniums, trades-cantias, English and Swedish ivies, coleus, African violets, pick-a-back, and pothos are some that root easily in water.

LEAF CUTTINGS—Leaves cut from certain plants, such as begonias or gloxinias, will produce young plants if several cuts are made with a sharp knife or a razor blade across the main veins before they are placed, right side up, on a rooting medium. Scatter moist sand on top or hold leaves down with toothpicks or small pegs so the cut veins will come in contact with the medium. Keep them moist. Cut off and pot the plantlets when they are well rooted and large enough to handle. Other plants adapted to this technique are African violets, watermelon begonia, sedums, and pick-a-back.

To increase humidity place a piece of polyethylene plastic over the containers with the cuttings. This will aid and also hasten rooting. Devise frameworks of wire for large pots and trays, or use a piece of wire screening to hold the plastic in position and thus achieve a green-house atmosphere. Always be careful not to overwater. The plastic holds in moisture, yet plants can breathe. Bell or brandy jars and inverted bottles are excellent to use. These are available at garden stores. Miniature greenhouses are neater than plastic contraptions and can be used continuously.

Some plants naturally produce offsets, runners, suckers, or stolons —that is, miniature plants along the sides of mother plants or at the tips of pendulous stems, as with spider plant(*Chlorophytum*). These usually root easily; some already have roots when disconnected. In this category are pick-a-back, screw pine or pandanus, strawberry begonia, apostle plant (*Neomarica*), haworthia, sempervivum (*hens-and-chickens*), and queen's tears (*Billbergia nutans*).

Many kinds of house plants are bulbous. Some of these are called technically rootstocks, corms, tubers, or rhizomes, but for general purposes the word "bulb" refers to all—amaryllis, agapanthus, clivia, hyacinth, tulip, nerine, freesia, Easter lily, gloriosa lily, caladium, crinum, calla, tuberous begonia, and veltheimia.

Air-layering a dumb cane: keeping the small cut open.

Watering the plastic-wrapped moss.

The newly formed root system.

The rooted and repotted plant.

When repotting bulbous plants, separate and pot the small bulbs along the sides of the old bulb. With some, such as lilies, bulblets appear at the axes of leaves. All bulbs are well supplied with nutrients and food, and make new plants easily. Large bulbs of some plants can be cut into smaller pieces, each with an eye, or sprout.

AIR-LAYERING—Another method is called air-layering (or Chinese or pot-layering), practiced largely on tall, leggy plants such as dracaena, dieffenbachia, rubber plant, aralia, schefflera, croton, and fiddle-leaved rubber plant (*Ficus pandurata*). Some of these do not root by cuttings.

At the desired point, usually eight to twelve inches from the tip, make an upward incision, one-third through the stem, with a sharp knife or razor blade. Insert a match stick, toothpick, or other small object in the cut to keep it open. Then surround the injured stem, where a callus will form (and hence roots), with a handful of moist sphagnum moss. Wrap with a piece of polyethylene plastic, wax paper, or tinfoil, and tie string around the stem at the bottom and top of the moss. Keep the top opening somewhat loose so you can apply water when the sphagnum moss becomes dry.

The sphagnum moss, when covered tightly, will remain moist for a long time, but do not allow it to dry out, as this will injure the new, young roots. When well filled with roots (they can be seen through transparent plastic), remove the plastic, cut the stem all the way through and pot the new plant in soil, leaving the sphagnum intact. The new plants may lose one or two lower leaves, but will soon start to grow.

Seeding is another method of propagation. It is the way to raise new varieties, such as the orange patient lucy (*Impatiens*) called Tangerine and the bicolored A Go-Go, wax begonias Jewelite and Christmas Candle, and coleus Chartreuse. New and exciting are the Fi Hybrid Carefree geraniums, which come true to type from seed. Free from most diseases, they are free branching, growing 18 inches tall, and all are vigorous and floriferous. They come in eight startling colors. Young plants can be set out in the garden and then brought indoors for the winter, or they can be kept in sunny windows all year round.

Another new strain of low-growing geraniums, called Little Big Shot, was introduced in 1971. Neat, vigorous, compact plants display small, dark green leaves and large flower heads, four inches across. Started from seed indoors, plants can be treated as permanent house plants or used in the garden. Colors include Little Big Shot Pink, Salmon, Red, and Scarlet (with white eye), and in mixtures. Seed for each color is available separately.

SEEDING MEDIUMS—Sow seeds in flats, tins, bulb pans, or indoor miniature greenhouses. Treat seed beforehand with a fungicide such as Semesan or Arasan (available at seed stores)—toss a pinch into the packet and shake thoroughly.

Scatter the seed on the moist medium or sow in neat rows, covering lightly with soil to twice the diameter of the seed. Once germinated, young seedlings should be fed with weak solutions of liquid fertilizer —one-fourth the recommended strength. Apply it when you are watering the tiny plants. Keep them at 65–70° F., with a drop of 5° to 10° at night. Give them sun to prevent lanky growth, and transplant the seedlings when the first true pairs of leaves appear—that is, those that are typical of the plant. Use individual pots or throw-away peat pots or bands. Square ones are especially useful because they fit snugly together and take up less space. Always keep moist; stems and leaves wilt if the plants are allowed to dry out, even for a day.

Effective propagating mediums (some have been mentioned elsewhere) include a mixture of 50–50 sharp, clean sand, and peatmoss or leafmold, and one-third sand, peatmoss or leafmold, and sterilized soil. Sand is good, but it dries quickly. Both vermiculite (heat-expanded mica) and perlite are excellent. They are sterile commercial products that remain well aerated and can be reused. Finely ground sphagnum moss—clean, sterile, and moisture retentive—is ideal for cuttings and seeds.

(8)

Bugs and Blights

Of all aspects of plant culture, indoors or out, dealing with bugs and blights is, for me, the most unpleasant. Not only does it require considerable know-how, but it takes constant effort to keep up with new scientific findings and products in the field. Though I could cheerfully do without spraying, I find it practically impossible to have healthy plants otherwise.

With spraying, if you do not know what you are doing, you do more harm than good. We are warned always to read directions carefully, but fail to do so in a moment of haste or laziness. Even I am guilty of this. When the pressurized aerosol bombs first came out, a friend asked me to use one for the white flies on her fuchsia. I sprayed too closely without reading the directions, with the result that the leaves and twigs were burned. Since then I have learned that the injury was caused by the presence of a freon, a chemical needed to keep the spray bomb pressurized. Spray bombs should be kept twelve to eighteen inches from the plants.

To look on the brighter side, indoor plants are not bothered with as many ailments as garden plants. Warm, dry air is ideal for insects, but not so good for diseases. Scale, mealy bugs, red spider mites, and aphids prevail, but hardly any mildew or leaf spot. Other fungi and viruses are not common, except for stem and root rotting, which are usually caused by oversaturated soil.

The best way to prevent maladies is to buy healthy plants in the beginning. Patronize reliable growers, and inspect each specimen carefully, examining leaf undersides and nodes where insects usually lurk. Yet, this is no guarantee. Boston ferns I once purchased broke out with scale, scheffleras were infested with red spider mites (detected with a magnifying glass), a Jerusalem cherry that came as a gift had aphids. I have brought home dumb canes plagued with mealy bugs, holly fern with scale, and geraniums with white flies. If possible spray all new house plants, a precautionary measure that always pays off.

Diseases (this term is used for both fungi and insects) spread easily from one plant to another. When you fondle your plants admiringly, you may unknowingly transfer red spider or aphids from one to the other. For this reason growers often forbid visitors to touch plants in display rooms. Sometimes it is better to throw out badly infected plants, especially stubborn cases that are difficult to control. This may seem heartless, but it takes a seasoned grower to develop this kind of philosophy. Avoid being sentimental, except for a large, heir-loom plant, like a Christmas cactus, camellia, agapanthus, epiphyllum, rubber plant, oleander, or sweet bay. A single plant can often infect an entire collection. Factors other than diseases may produce a weakened, yellow condition—overwatering, underwatering, chilling, lack of nourishment, or insufficient light.

COMMON PESTS—The most common insect pests on house plants are aphids, mealy bugs, scale, red spider mites, and white flies, which you may know by name but not by appearance.

Aphids, or plant lice, are small soft-bodied insects, winged or wingless, according to stage of development, that give birth to young. They harm plants by sucking juices, especially tender growth, causing leaves and stems to wrinkle. Aphids give off a colorless secretion known as honeydew, the sticky substance that "rains" down on the windshield of cars from street trees in summer. A popular misconception is that trees are giving off sap. Fond of many kinds of house plants, including English ivies, coleus, and patience plant, aphids are notorious disease carriers. If only a few are present, wash plants under the faucet, using your finger tips to help dislodge them. Or spray with the old-time nicotine sulphate (Black Leaf 40), malathion (it has an unpleasant odor), or thiodan.

Mealy bugs, which frequently appear on African violets, English ivies, begonias, ferns, coleus, fuchsias, and gardenias, are flat, segmented, oval insects, one-fourth inch long, resembling bits of cotton fluff. They like warmth, and feed on plant sap. Usually they congregate in colonies at the axils of branches or along the veins on undersides of leaves. The cottony fluff represents the egg sacs on females. If mealy bugs are few, they can be picked off by hand or washed away under a strong force of faucet water. You can also eliminate them with a small swab of cotton rolled around the end of a toothpick, immersed in rubbing alcohol, nail polish, or witch-hazel. Or you can spray plants with nicotine sulphate or malathion.

The most stubborn insect, scale, usually appears as oval encrustations. Varying in size and shape, they may have hard or soft shells and may be brown, black, or white in coloring. Like aphids and mealy bugs, scales are sucking insects. A shell protects them in the adult stage; the eggs are laid by females before they die. A few scales on a plant can be rubbed off with the fingernails or killed with the cotton-tipped toothpick dabbed in rubbing alcohol. On a large plant, this can be tedious and next to impossible. Spray with diazinon or malathion, making three or four applications, but repeat as often as is necessary. Best control is effected when crawlers are present, that is, the young before they develop a hard shell. Scale is usually found on plants with smooth leaf surfaces—palms, lemons, oranges and other citrus, gardenias, camellias, hoyas, peperomias, and ferns, where it is notoriously a problem. Since ferns are sensitive to many chemicals in emulsifiable form, use only wettable powders such as wettable malathion, which is also a remedy for mealy bugs.

Red spiders are not true spiders, but rather mites (animals) with four pairs of legs. They are so tiny, they are hardly visible to the naked eye. A magnifying glass is usually needed to detect them. Red spider mite and cyclamen mite are the most common kinds. Telltale evidence of red spider mites, also called two-spotted mites, are a dusty, yellowish, grayish appearance of leaves, as well as webbing on the undersurfaces. They are common on English ivies and schffleras. Over a piece of white paper shake a plant that is suspected of infection and the mites will drop as tiny specks. You can also discover them with a magnifying glass as they scurry about on the undersides of leaves.

Mites often cause considerable damage before they are detected. Leaves will turn yellow or dry up and drop, and entire plants will become sickly, seemingly overnight. Red spider mites enjoy hot, dry atmospheres (the average apartment and home is an incubator), and dislike high humidity and good air ventilation. Since they are easily dislodged, remove them by washing the undersides of leaves two or three times a week. Or use a convenient pressurized bomb. Kelthane and tedion give excellent control.

Cyclamen mite, a near relative of red spider mite, is far more insidious. As its name suggests, it has a penchant for cyclamen, but attacks African violets, delphiniums, chrysanthemums, and snapdragons in the garden. White or green in coloring, it is microscopic and cannot be seen with the naked eye. Cyclamen mites feed on the growing tips of plants, including buds and flowers, causing them to become stunted, twisted, wrinkled, anf gray or black in coloring. Leaves are curly or distorted, Cut out infested parts and destroy, then spray the plant with kelthane or thiodan. It is sometimes necessary to throw away badly infested plants. Since cyclamen mite is easily transferred, wash your hands thoroughly after handling an ailing specimen.

White fly is another difficult-to-control insect. A small, white, winged fly that sucks plant juices, it usually congregates on the undersides of leaves, causing them to turn yellow, wilt, and die. When plants are disturbed, they fly out, but return later. The young, which look like small green dots, are wingless and can be washed off, but for adults, use malathion or diazinon. White flies are especially attracted to fuchsias, heliotropes, and geraniums, and may be transferred to gardens from greenhouse stock. Control with malathion.

THRIPS are equally undesirable. They are minute insects hardly to be detected with the naked eye. There are many kinds, but gladiolus thrips is the best known. Thrips are found in colonies. They suck plant juices, leaving silvery or white specks that give foliage, flowers, and stems a dotted appearance. Leaves become papery and wilt. Thrips can be killed with malathion, but are also discouraged by a dry atmosphere.

OTHER PROBLEMS Leaf miners are small insects that live and feed between leaf surfaces. They are well named, because they leave visible white serpentine markings, tunnels, or runways on the leaves. Less common than other pests on house plants, they are found on potted azaleas, chrysanthemums, palms, and tender hollies. Cut off and destroy infested leaves or spray plants with malathion or diazinon. Follow instructions carefully, since timing is very important.

Occasionally you may find slugs and snails among your pot plants, usually brought indoors in the fall in pots that were plunged in the open ground during the summer. Sometimes they are present in the soil moisture. These are very unpleasant creatures that leave a slimy trail behind them, as they chew holes and devour large areas of leaves —especially the most succulent. Slugs and snails travel at night, and indoors are apt to be found in planters. They can easily be discovered with a flashlight. You may find a small, hard-shelled snail, an inch or more in diameter, or a soft, slimy slug, which is a snail without a shell. Both have two blunt horns on their heads. You can control them with a poison bait containing methaldehyde. Use it according to manufacturer's directions. Also pick off and destroy (with gloves if you are squeamish) all you find. Slugs and snails in the soil injure roots, severing them if they are fine and disrupting their contact with the soil.

Earthworms are easily detected by their droppings: dark brown lumps on the surface of the pot soil. To get rid of the worms, remove plants from their pots, and work the soil gently until they drop out. As a youngster, I remember watering my house plants with a solution of water and ammonia to induce earthworms to crawl through the drainage openings. A teaspoonful of dry mustard dissolved in a gallon of water will do the same.

Sometimes small, wingless, fast-moving insects appear on the surface of the soil. Called springtails, they are generally harmless insects that feed on decayed organic matter. A large number of them, however, will damage the small, fibrous, feeding roots of plants and also deprive them of nourishment. You can control springtails by spraying the soil and lower portions of plants with malathion.

Diseases

Mildew is one of the few diseases found on house plants. It is a white mold that covers leaf surfaces with whitish powder. Fostered by warm, humid conditions, it is not likely to appear outside of conservatories or greenhouses. It can be checked with sulphur or karathane, both of which are fungicides that leave a residue.

Rotting of plant stems near the base is caused by disease spores favored by conditions of excessive watering. Like mildew, it is not common where the air is hot and dry. Stems above the rotted portions wither and die, because the moisture supply is cut off. This occurs frequently on heart-leaved philodendron. Avoid overwatering, and cut out affected portions. In extreme cases, toss out the entire plant because roots have rotted.

When green leaves drop for no apparent reason (it happens frequently to heart-leaved philodendron), it is because an abscission layer forms between the stem and petiole. Several factors may be to blame —lack of humidity, chilling, quick changes in temperature, drying out, decreased light, change in the period of light, overwatering, or destruction of most of the leaf area. In any case, it is most disconcerting for green leaves to drop to the floor overnight or even before your eyes when you touch them gently.

Spray carefully. The easiest way to enjoy healthy house plants is to spray them periodically for pests and diseases with an all around combination that contains methoxychlor, malathion, kelthane, and captan. Always take extra effort to heed the manufacturer's advice on aerosol bombs, holding them twelve to eighteen inches away; if they are held closer, the gas (needed for pressure) will "freeze" or burn the leaves. Spray with a rotary motion and make several applications. Two kinds of chemical sprays are available: wettable powders that may leave an unsightly residue (which many will find objectionable), and emulsifiable sprays.

Store your insecticides in a cool, dry place. Emulsifiable insecticide formulas will break down in freezing weather, so do not keep them in heated garages or sheds in winter. Wettable powders possess limited effectiveness, and this is evident when they begin to lump or "ball." Malathion, for example, keeps well for six months to a year (in an all-purpose combination, the other chemicals remain effective, too); kelthane, two years; sevin, two years; and zineb, one year. Sulphur, ferbam, captan, and karathane are all very suitable fungicides that keep a long time.

Promising New Pest Control

Now becoming available—and much easier to apply—are systemic insecticides for house plants. These are recommended only for the control of sucking insects; aphids, spider mites, white flies, leaf miners, and certain other pests. Scattered on the soil, they are scratched in, and then watered in. The insecticide enters a plant through its roots and works its way through the stems and into the leaves. One I tried—for the first time—resembled multi-hued sand and gave off a rather unpleasant odor that lasted a day or two. The directions were to use a heaping teasonful for a four-inch pot, two for six- or eight-inch pots, and three for eight- or ten-inch pots. Be certain, in every case, to follow instructions with great care as outlined on the package of the systemic insecticide you buy for your house plants. Actually, this represents a revolution in the realm of spraying house plants, as it did in outdoor gardens, one that promises to be a great boon to indoor gardeners.

When in doubt about pests, diseases and controls, consult your Agricultural Experiment Station—every state has at least one. Your nurseryman or garden center can often be of assistance, too, especially if staffed by knowledgeable experienced horticulturists. Always rely on manufacturers' instructions and be sure to read the fine print on containers.

Sometimes house plant failure is due to cooking gas. The old-time artificial gas was definitely harmful to house plants: geraniums would not bloom, Jerusalem cherries would drop their fruits, carnation blossoms would fold up and go to sleep, while leaves of several kinds of house plants would turn yellow. Fortunately, natural gas does not have an injurious effect on plants.

(9)

Plants in Pots, Planters and Room Dividers

A pot, or a container, is the receptacle in which a house plant grows. The word "pot" designates a vessel that holds soil for plant roots. Pot shapes may be oval, square, rectangular, octagonal, or free-form. Materials for pots vary equally. Most common is the traditional clay or earthenware pot—at least it was until plastic came along. Others are made from fiberglass, copper, iron, and other metals, plus a host of new synthetic materials.

Puzzling to beginners are such terms as two-, three-, or four-inch pot, and bulb and azalea pan. Actually, pot size is measured by its diameter across the top. When it is equally tall and wide, it is known as a standard or regular pot, the kind most frequently used. A bulb pan is half as tall as it is wide, and is used chiefly for hyacinths, daffodils, and other bulbs. It is wide enough for several bulbs to be grouped closely in it for spectacular effects.

An azalea pot, three-fourths as tall as wide, is preferred by growers for shrubbery azaleas, Cyclamen is usually raised in a cyclamen pot, three-fifths as high as broad; a rose pot, deeper than wide, accommodates the long root systems of roses. As pots become larger, they increase in diameter at the rate of one inch per size, and usually increase proportionately in depth.

When repotting your house plants, keep in mind their ultimate height. For most plants, such as geraniums, begonias, coleus, philodendrons, dumb canes, and other foliage types, choose the standard pot. For a single hyacinth or daffodil, select a three- or four-inch azalea pot, rather than a bulb pan because it is in better proportion. Three or five hyacinths, tulips, or other bulbs require a six-inch bulb pan, but seven bulbs will take the next larger size.

After size, consider the pot material carefully. Soil dries out quicker in porous pots than in those made of impervious substances. Some pots break easily, others crumble only when hit hard. Keep weight in mind, as well as overall general appearance.

CLAY POTS—The familiar unglazed clay pot comes in many sizes. Not particularly ornamental, it is inexpensive and readily obtainable, harmonizing with all colors. It is "raw" looking when new, but mellows with time.Clay containers are porous, and dry out quickly in high temperatures. Unless specially treated, they gather moss and fertilizer salts on the outside, which detracts from their appearance. Clean with a stiff brush dipped in warm, soapy water before potting, and periodically thereafter, as needed. Clay pots last for years. They break easily when hit or dropped, but are inexpensive, and the pieces can be saved for crocks to be used over and over again as drainage material.

More decorative are glazed earthenware pots, available in an infinite variety of shapes, sizes, and colors. The glaze prevents mosses and fertilizer salts from accumulating on the outside. These containers hold moisture longer, and are usually more expensive. Though many glazed containers lack drainage holes, plants can be grown in them successfully if a thick layer of drainage material, usually one-third the height of the container, is placed at the bottom to catch excess water. Always water with extra caution. Glazed pots with floral or geometric patterns are best suited to foliage plants; use containers of solid colors for flowering plants.

PLASTIC POTS—Nowadays, most pots are made of plastic. Recently introduced, they range widely in size and shape; colors may be green, gray, black, buff, brown, or white—often heavily streaked or mottled. Many prefer them to clay, but I am not one of their advocates. Nonporous, they hold moisture in the soil longer than clay. If watering is watched carefully, this is an advantage; if not, plants are harmed by overwatering. Economical, light in weight, durable, and clean, they do not break easily. However, larger sizes will sometimes crack at the rim if lifted from one side; this is caused by the uneven distribution of weight, especially when soil is moist or wet.

WOODEN TUBS—Wooden tubs or buckets are offered in large sizes, and often prove to be the only solution for large rubber plants, oleanders, camellias, clivias, agapanthus, Chinese hibiscus, Norfolk-Island-pines, jade plants, and orchid cactus. In summer they adorn terraces, porches, steps, walks, and lawns handsomely. Wooden tubs are heavy, durable, and long lasting if treated with a wood preservative. Those purchased at garden centers and nurseries have usually been treated. Redwood, cedar and cypress tubs and boxes do not require treatment because they are naturally long lasting. If you construct your own boxes with other kinds of woods, use Cuprinol, a preservative that is nontoxic to plants, and paint them to improve appearance. Allow redwood, cypress, and cedar to mellow naturally.

Pots, tubs, and other containers require saucers to catch drainage water. Plastic ones are inexpensive, nonbreakable, and impervious to water. Colors include green, black, gray, and white in sizes large enough for tubs and buckets. Some treated clay saucers are also impervious to water.

Jardinieres conceal unsightly soiled clay and plastic pots. They last long, so buy good ones. Think of them as objets d'art that add to the decor of your rooms. I prefer soft, subtle colorings—white, creamy-white, gold, yellow, beige, light blue, and all shades of green. Place leather mats or coasters under jardinieres to avoid scratching furniture. Or glue them on the bottoms of jardinieres. Jardinieres and other pot covers come in other materials as well—copper, brass, iron and other metals, plastic, fiberglass, and numerous synthetic products, usually nonbreakable and light in weight.

BASKETS—There is a trend toward baskets, especially those suited to traditional and contemporary interiors, and they come in a variety of weaves; the handmade are the most durable. Many gardeners like to collect baskets as they do jardinieres—I for one. Handsome and nonbreakable, they comprise a permanent investment to be handed down to family or given to friends.

Plan to use jardinieres and baskets that cover pots completely. Pots that protrude much above the tops are aesthetically jarring. Take a tape measure when you go shopping; a slightly large jardiniere or basket is better than one that is too small.

Always water plants in jardinieres with extreme caution. If water drains through, empty the excess as soon as draining ceases. Better still, place a layer of pebbles or an inverted plastic saucer or old kitchen dish inside the jardiniere so the pots will not rest in drainage water. For this, select jardinieres that are extra large. When you have acquired a sizeable collection of jardinieres and baskets, you can move them from plant to plant to create new effects. Keep them clean, and store them carefully when they are not in use, as in summer when plants are outdoors.

PLANTERS AND ROOM DIVIDERS—There is a feeling of stability given by planters and room dividers in which foliage plants and others are grown. In today's houses, especially those of contemporary design, these large containers are striking decorative features. New houses are often equipped with built in planters, placed either across a large picture window, along an entrance wall or as dividers between the kitchen and living room areas. This is quite usual today in city apartments.

Such large containers are constructed to harmonize with room interiors, often separating rooms into smaller units. Sometimes planters, one to four feet high, are built into the ground on the first floor—in a vestibule or "well," with light streaming in from above or from one or more sides. The effect is enchanting, somewhat like a Roman atrium where large plants such as palms, scheffleras, aralias, citrus, hibiscus, avocados, dracaenas, monsteras, rubber plants, and crotons, are allowed free root run. They are inviting green oases, where seasonal plants such as poinsettias, cyclamen, hydrangeas, and spring bulbs can be added for color. However, these are generally more common in motels, office buildings, and other places of business.

But most planters, movable or not, have limited root runs. Variable in form—square, rectangular, triangular, circular, or free-form—they are constructed of many kinds of materials. These include nondecaying woods such as cedar, cypress, and redwood; ordinary woods like white pine, which must be treated with a nontoxic preservative to prevent quick decay; metals; plastic; fiberglass; and other synthetic products. Planters last longer if the insides are lined with galvanized sheet metal or with copper, brass, stainless steel, or plastic. Make certain they are deep enough to hold sufficient amounts of soil or deep enough for the pots to be held. At the bottom place two to four inches of gravel, charcoal, pebbles, or broken crocks to catch excess water. Six- to eight-inch pots need planters that are twelve to fifteen inches deep; smaller pots, three to five inches, require a depth of six to nine inches. Be sure the height of plants is in proportion to the depth of planters.

PLANTS IN PLANTERS—There are three different ways to handle plants in planters. The first is to leave them in their pots and fill around them with peatmoss, perlite, crushed stone, or other material. The second is to place pots directly on a layer of pebbles or stones, without covering them. The third is to remove plants from their pots and set them in the soil.

The first method is generally considered the most practical. Concealed with peatmoss or other medium, plants give the illusion of growing in soil. Yet they can be turned around, removed for repotting or spraying, or rearranged without one disturbing the other. Sickly or overlarge specimens can be removed and replaced, and flowering kinds can be rotated to add holiday color. Left in their pots, plant roots are confined without becoming entangled, but derive moisture from the surrounding medium, particularly if the pots are ceramic.

The second method offers other advantages. Each plant can be given similar individual attention, and can be removed more easily than if imbedded in a medium. The water level in the layer on which pots rest can be watched. If large plants are placed closely enough, their pots can be concealed with low-growing fillers such as English, kangaroo, and Swedish ivies; aluminum plants, philodendrons, pothos, asparagus ferns, and inch plants.

On the whole, the third method is the least desirable. Planted in deep, well-prepared soil, plants enjoy a freer root run and grow better, but disadvantages are obvious. Sickly or overgrown specimens, for example cannot be taken out without injuring or cutting the roots of other plants. They cannot be removed to be sprayed, nor turned around if they are becoming one-sided. Usually, the tougher, faster-growing, or more vigorous plants will take over, crowding out, or killing the less aggressive sorts.

PLACING OF PLANTERS—No hard and fast rules dictate the placement of planters. Locate wherever they look best—to soften a bare wall, create a degree of privacy in a large room, or add a friendly, colorful touch. The entrance often provides an excellent setting for one or more planters, where they greet visitors with warmth and set the mood for the rest of the house or apartment. If possible, locate movable planters near large windows for good light, but transfer them from one room to another for parties. Planters may be placed in large bathrooms. And movable planters may be transferred to the terrace or porch, set under large trees during the summer.

Plants in planters need the same care as other house plants. Provide good natural light or give them artificial lighting, if needed; water when the soil surface becomes dry. Imbedded pots stay moist for several days, so learn to probe with your fingers through the medium to determine moisture needs. Feed mostly during the spring-to-autumn growing period. With a damp sponge or cloth, wipe dust from leaf surfaces. Use a mist spray to increase humidity; remove yellow leaves and prune, pinch or cut off leggy growth. If pots rest on pebbles or stones, keep adding water as some will be lost in evaporation.

When arranging plants, graduate them according to height, using the tallest in the back, medium-height, in the center, and short ones, including trailers, along the front. Introduce a few variegated-leaved kinds to break the monotony of solid green. Plants with leaves of varying sizes and textures make interesting contrasts in composing a plant picture. Small pots may be propped on wooden blocks or set on inverted pots to bring them to the desired level. Arrange these me-chanics before filling in around pots with the medium selected, keep-ing any aids as inconspicuous as possible. Remember that small, spreading or trailing plants are excellent concealments when used as ground covers around the bases of tall and leggy foliage plants and flowering specimens.

GLOSSARY OF PLANT TERMS

Acid-loving—A term used to refer to a plant that requires an acid soil condition, such as azalea, gardenia, and camellia.

Aerial roots—Roots appearing on plant stems or branches, often used for support on walls, such as English ivy and philodendron.

Agricultural lime—Ground limestone; slower acting and more lasting than hydrated or burned lime, which are so strong they tend to destroy humus in the soil.

Air-layering—A method of propagating hard-to-root plants, such as croton and rubber plant; also known as Chinese air-layering.

Alkaline—A term used to refer to a plant that requires a non-acid soil condition, such as carnation, stock, etc.

Annual—A plant which usually completes its life cycle—from seed to seed—in one growing season.

Axil—The angle formed by the joining of a leaf stem to a twig or branch and the stem to which it is attached.

Bare-rooted—A term used to refer to a plant that is sold or handled with no soil around its roots.

Biennial—A plant that produces its flowers and seeds in its second year and then dies.

Bonemeal—A slow-acting fertilizer composed of crushed or finely ground animal bones; supplies mainly phosphorus and a small amount of nitrogen.

Bract—A modified leaf, often highly colored, around the smaller, inconspicuous true flowers, as seen in poinsettia and bougainvillea.

Bud-dropping—A term that refers to the release and falling of flower buds before they open; common with cammellia and gardenia when growing conditions are unfavorable.

Bulb—A swollen underground stem (not root) that has the capacity to store food for future foliage and flowers. The term is used generally to include true bulbs often loosely applied to others that are "bulbous," such as canna (rhizome), gladiolus (corm), and tuberous begonia (which is a tuber), which see.

Bulbous—A plant having a true bulb (which see) such as tulip, lily, etc., or a similar stem or root swelling that may more properly be termed corm, rhizome, or tuber.

Charcoal—Crushed bits of partially-burned hardwood used to sweeten sour soil and to keep water clean, thus recommended for plants grown in water.

Compost—Decomposed vegetable matter mixed with fertilizer and lime; used for potting or mulching.

Compound leaf—One made up of leaflets, as seen in the rose, grape ivy, schefflera, etc.

Corm—A solid, bulb-like, subterranean stem, without scales; with the leaves developing from the prominent terminal bud, as found in crocus, gladiolus, tigridia, etc.

Crock or Crocks—Pieces of broken earthenware containers, clay flowerpots and the like, used as drainage material above bottom openings of pots.

Cutting—A section of a plant, including a portion of the stem, taken for propagation.

Deciduous—A plant that sheds its leaves during the autumn, such as an elm or maple tree; the opposite of evergreen.

Disbud—The process of removing buds, usually those below the terminal bud at the top, so that the remaining bud or buds will put all energy into producing larger blossoms.

Division—A section of a plant, pulled apart or cut with a knife or spade, for propagation, as practiced with snake plant and aspidistra.

Dormant—A term applied to a plant that is not in active growth, usually because of a natural period of rest, as seen in winter in cold climates.

Epiphyte—A plant which in nature grows upon another, usually rooting in decayed vegetable matter as found in the crotch of a tree, for instance, but not parasitic. Orchid is an outstanding example.

Evergreen—A plant which retains its foliage throughout the year; the opposite of deciduous.

Fibrous-rooted—A term that refers to plants with many fine thread-like roots, creating fibrous root systems, such as African violets, begonias, etc.

Force—A term applied when plants are made to bloom out of season; for instance, daffodils and tulips in January and February, chrysanthemums the year round.

Frond—Usually the leaf of a fern, though it can be the leaves of some other plants, such as palms.

Fungicide—Any substance that will kill fungi and bacteria in plants, seeds, or soil or check the development of spores. The most common fungicides are compounded of sulphur or copper, and may be dry or soluble in liquids.

Genus—A subdivision of a plant family, which in turn is made up of other divisions known as species. The genus name begins with a capital letter, the species is in lower case letters. *Philodendron cordata* is an example.

Hardwood cutting—One severed from a fully matured shoot, usually of the current year's growth, such as the firm stem of a camellia.

Herb—In common use, it usually refers to a plant used for culinary, medicinal or cosmetic purposes. In botany it is used in a wider sense. See Herbaceous.

Herbaceous—A plant with little or no persistent woody tissue, one that usually lasts only a single growing season, although the roots, crown, bulb or whizome survives to throw up new growth the next year.

Hormone powder—Synthetic chemicals such as idelobutyric and naphthalene-acetamide, that are used to induce cuttings to root earlier and to produce a greater number of roots.

Hybrid—The crossing of plants of two different genera to produce another, mingling the two characteristics.

Inorganic matter—Material that is not composed of organic matter, like plants and animals. In horticulture the term is often used to describe chemical fertilizers and mulches such as pebbles and stones.

Kelthane—A chemical, miticide, used to control red spider and other mites.

Lath house—A structure constructed of laths or slats, allowing filtered sun and air to reach the plants grown under it.

Leaf cutting—A piece of a leaf or an entire leaf, with or without its leaf stalk, that is used to propagate plants. Fleshy leaves, such as African violet or peperomia, are best propagated by this method.

Leaf mold—The humusy residue of partially or wholly decomposed leaves.

Leggy—Describing a plant that has lost its lower leaves and lower stems have become bare, although tops may be vigorous.

Linear—A term used to refer to a leaf that is long and slender, such as that of agapanthus or twelve apostles.

Lobed—A term referring to leaves that have divisions that extend to the center or almost to the base, such as the leaf of a maple or English ivy.

Long-day plant—One that waits for the period of long days and short nights to set its flower buds.

Malathion—An organic phosphate of relatively low toxicity to mammals that is used as wide spectrum insecticide.

Miticide—A chemical used to control plant mites, such as red spider mite.

Nicotine sulfate—A contact insecticide, containing 40% nicotine, useful for control of aphids and thrips, usually sold under the trade name of Black Leaf 40.

Node—The joint or knob on a stem from which a bud or leaf may start to grow.

Notched—A term used to describe a concave or V-shaped cut made in a stem in the air-layering method of propagation.

Offset—A side shoot that takes root and starts a new plant, similar to a runner but with a shorter stem, as found on the American century plant (agave).

Opposite leaves—Those that appear in pairs on side of opposite plant stems.

Organic matter—Decomposed material that once had life, derived from plants and animals.

Osmunda fiber—The fibrous roots of the osmunda fern, which when dug, chopped, and dried, are used for the growing of orchids.

Overpot—To give a house plant a pot that is too large for its present needs; undesirable because soil does not dry out quickly enough.

Peatmoss—The decomposed, or partially decomposed matter of sphagnum or other moss, sedges, and other plants of bog areas. Used as a rooting medium or mulch, also to provide humus in soil mixtures.

Perennial—A plant which lives several years. Some perennials are woody stemmed. See also Herbaceous.

Perlite—A light, gritty, inert material used as a substitute for sand in potting mixtures. Also used as a sterile medium for sowing seed, rooting cuttings, aerating soil, and for storing bulbs in. Also employed as a mulch.

Petiole—The stem or stalk of a leaf.

Pinch, Pinch out—To remove the growing tip of a plant with scissors, knife, or the finger tips in order to make it branch out and become bushier.

Pistil—The complete female organ of reproduction of a flowering plant; the part that bears the ovary and the seed.

Plunge—To sink a plant outdoors in the open ground in its pot or to put it in a basin to absorb water when soil becomes dry.

Pollen—The male element in a flower that fertilizes the ovule. It is borne on the anther, is usually dust-like and yellow in color.

Polyethylene plastic—A kind of plastic film, available in sheets or as bags. It is permeable by air but retentive of moisture and is used as a cover for cuttings in rooting mediums to hold in moisture and humidity, also to bag plants on vacation.

Potbound—A condition whereby a pot plant is so filled with roots that little or no area remains for their development.

Prune—To trim a plant, to cut or lop off dead, weak, and superfluous growth in order to shape and improve its appearance and promote its vigor.

Rhizome—See *Rootstock*

Rooting medium—Any material used for rooting plants: soil, sand, peatmoss, perlite, vermiculite, sphagnum moss, and water, are used, some are better than others for specific plants.

Rootstock—A swollen, usually elongated underground stem of a perennial herb, such as iris, often called rhizome by botanists. Also, the base of a plant on which cutting is grafted to form a new top.

Rosette—A cluster of leaves or petals radiating symmetrically from the center.

Runner—A plant shoot that trails along the ground, rooting at the joints, as seen in wandering Jew, or a shoot at the end of which a small plant develops, as with spider plant (chlorophytum) or strawberry begonia.

Species—A subdivision of the plant group known as genus, designating a particular kind, usually one as found in nature, like *Hoya carnosa*.

Softwood cutting—One made from stem tips, usually soft and immature or green and pliable, as with coleus or patience plant.

Short-day plant—One that needs a period of short days and long nights in order to set its flower buds; for example, chrysanthemum and Christmas cactus.

Sphagnum or sphagnum moss—Highly absorbent, graying mosses found in bogs; dried, it is used in soil mixtures and for propagation purposes.

Stamen—The pollen-bearing male organ of a flower, made up of a slender stalk and a pollen sac.

Stolon—A slender horizontal stem occurring just above or below the ground, that roots at the joints or tips, such as those of strawberry begonia when grown in the open ground.

Succulent—A plant made up of leaf, stem, and root parts that have the capacity to hold water and are therefore drought-resistant. Cactus is the outstanding example.

Sucker—A secondary shoot growing from the rootstock, the lower part of the trunk or below ground level, usually at the expense of the mother plant.

Superphosphate—A fertilizer comprised of 20% phosphorus which, unlike bon-meal, does not contain nitrogen.

Tuber—A thickened portion of an underground stem or branch that is provided with "eyes," as seen in the dahlia and tuberous-rooted begonia.

Trailer—A plant that in its native habitat trails or straggles along the ground. Because of this characteristic, these can be grown in a hanging basket.

Tendril—The thread-like part of a climbing plant, often coiling, by means of which it climbs, as found in grape ivy, passion plant, clematis, etc.

Tender—Usually a plant tropical or subtropical in origin, one unable to survive temperatures below 32 degrees or even somewhat higher ones. If it does survive, it may become nipped or injured above ground.

Variety—A subdivision of plant nomenclature, usually a variation of a species, either whether it occurs naturally or has been consciously developed by a plant breeder.

Vermiculite—A light, inert, gritty, long-lasting micaceous material used in place of sand in potting plants and for sowing seed and rooting cuttings, as well as in aerating soil. It can also be used as a medium in which to store bulbs.

Whorl—A circular growth of stems, petals, or leaves radiating around a particular point on a stem, seen in the branching habit of the Norfolk-Island-pine, for instance.

INDEX